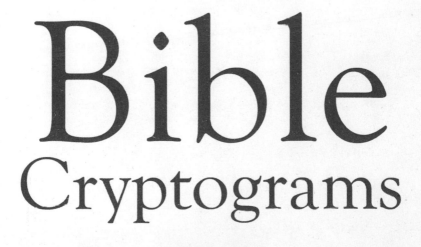

10 Spiritual Fruit

VLVJ YP VLVCI TPPG BCVV ZCSJTVBD KPCBD TPPG

KCMSB; ZMB X QPCCMAB BCVV ZCSJTVBD KPCBD VLSR

KCMSB.

FXBBDVU 7:17   *Clue: T = G*

_____

GAU WFY GHCWE SXNH TBHH TBFS RCW, XWN

GHQFSH RHBIXWUR UF EFN, LH OXIH LFAB TBACU AWUF

OFJCWHRR, XWN UOH HWN HIHBJXRUCWE JCTH.

BFSXWR 6:22   *Clue: G = B*

404
All-New
Challenging
Puzzles

Bible
Cryptograms

BARBOUR
PUBLISHING

P9-DIJ-814

© 2009 by Barbour Publishing, Inc.

Puzzles edited by Jennifer Hahn.

ISBN 978-1-60260-350-9

All rights reserved. No part of this publication may be reproduced or transmitted for commercial purposes, except for brief quotations in printed reviews, without written permission of the publisher.

Churches and other noncommercial interests may reproduce portions of this book without the express written permission of Barbour Publishing, within the following limitations: no more than one puzzle per month in a physical publication made for free distribution (for example, church bulletins, club newsletters, etc.). When reproducing text from this book, include the following credit line: "From *Bible Cryptograms*, published by Barbour Publishing, Inc. Used by permission." Puzzles may not be reproduced electronically.

All scripture quotations are taken from the King James Version of the Bible.

Published by Barbour Publishing, Inc., P.O. Box 719, Uhrichsville, Ohio 44683 www.barbourbooks.com

Our mission is to publish and distribute inspirational products offering exceptional value and biblical encouragement to the masses.

ecpa Member of the
Evangelical Christian
Publishers Association

Printed in the United States of America.

Welcome to Bible Crytograms!

If you like Bible cryptograms, you'll love this book. Here are 404 brand-new puzzles to expand your Bible knowledge and test your puzzle-solving skills, as thousands of encoded letters—all in verses taken from the King James Version of the Bible—await you.

Each cryptogram is a verse in a substitution code. For example, JEHOVAH might become MPXSTQX if M is substituted for J, P for E, X for H, and so on. One way to break the code is to look for repeated letters: E, T, A, O, N, R, and I are the most often used. Single letters are usually A or I, and OF, IT, and IS are common two-letter words. Try THE and AND for three-letter groups. The puzzle titles and the scripture references may give you additional direction, and—if you want even more help—we've provided a substitution clue with each puzzle. Remember that the code is different for each Bible cryptogram. Answers begin on page 206.

We know you're eager to get started, so just one final word: Enjoy!

1 Born Again!

FOR I AM NOT ASHAMED OF THE GOSPEL of
ZGB Q OH YGC OVJOHKR GZ CJK LGVFKS GZ

CHRIST FOR IT IS THE POWER OF GOD UNTO
WJBQVC: ZGB QC QV CJK FGMKB GZ LGR NYCG

SALVATION TO EVERY ONE THAT BELIEVETH TO THE
VOSXOCQGY CG KXBI GYK CJOC AKSQKXKCJ; CG CJK

JEW FIRST AND A SO TO THE GREEK
TKM ZQBVC, OYR OSVG CG CJK LBKKP.

ROMANS
BGHOYV 1:16

Clue: L = G

BUT WE ARE BOUNDTO GIVE THANKS ALWAY TO
KGF YA PHA KUGJE FU RXNA FMPJQW PBYPC FU

GOD FOR YOU BRETHREN BELOVED OF THE LORD
RUE VUH CUG, KHAFMHAJ KABUNAE UV FMA BUHE,

BECAUSE GOD HATH FROM THE BEGINNING CHOSEN
KATPGWA RUE MPFM VHUD FMA KARXJJXJR TMUWAJ

YOU TO SALVATION THROUGH SANCTIFICATION OF
CUG FU WPBNPFXUJ FMHUGRM WPJTFXVXTPFXUJ UV

THE SPIRIT AND BELIEF OF THE TRUTH
FMA WZXHXF PJE KABXAV UV FMA FHGFM.

2 FMAWWPBUJXPJW 2:13
THES SALONIHANS

Clue: C = Y

2 The Key Ingredient

AND JESUS SAID UNTO HIM GO THY WAY

URM ATGZG GUVM ZRHN QVK, CN HQD FUD;

THY FAITH HATH MADE THEE WHOLE AND

HQD IUVHQ QUHQ KUMT HQTT FQNOT. URM

IMMEDIATELY HE RECEIVED HIS SIGHT AND

VKKTMVUHTOD QT JTETVLTM QVG GVCQH, URM

FOLLOWED JESUS IN THE WAY

INOONFTM ATGZG VR HQT FUD.

KUJX 10:52   *Clue: O = I*

MARK

FOR THEREIN IS THE RIGHTEOUSNESS OF

KUG CYVGVXW XL CYV GXHYCVUQLWVLL UK

GOD REVEALED FROM FAITH TO FAITH AS IT IS

HUB GVPVRDVB KGUS KRXCY CU KRXCY: RL XC XL

WRITTEN THE JUST SHALL LIVE BY FAITH

JGXCCVW, CYV TQLC LYRDD DXPV OF KRXCY.

ROMANS

GUSRWL 1:17   *Clue: Y = H*

3) A Wing and a Prayer

OUR SOUL IS ESCAPED AS A BIRD OUT OF THE SNARE
CVZ RCVU GR BRQFDBX FR F LGZX CVE CK ESB RMFZB

OF THE FOWLERS THE SNARE IS BROKEN AND WE ARE
CK ESB KCHUBZR: ESB RMFZB GR LZCNBM, FMX HB FZB

ESCAPED
BRQFDBX.

PSALM
DRFUA 124:7   *Clue: V = U*

CURSE NOT THE KING NO NOT IN THY THOUGHT AND
TDVOL ERA AJL GKEF, ER ERA KE AJU AJRDFJA; NES

CURSE NOT THE RICH IN THY BEDCHAMBER FOR A BIRD
TDVOL ERA AJL VKTJ KE AJU HLSTJNPHLV: MRV N HKVS

OF THE AIR SHALL CARRY THE VOICE AND THAT WHICH
RM AJL NKV OJNXX TNVVU AJL ZRKTL, NES AJNA BJKTJ

HATH WINGS SHALL TELL THE MATTER
JNAJ BKEFO OJNXX ALXX AJL PNAALV.

ECCLESIASTES
LTTXLOKNOALO 10:20   *Clue: F = G*

4) A Very Important Person

ZLC JRV URXEC FWVB, ZLC PRV YWITFRJ RXO TLJI

KRZWZIR'P CZTFRJVW, ZLC RV YVUZOV RVW PIL. ZLC

PRV UZEEVC RXP LZOV OIPVP: ZLC PRV PZXC, YVUZTPV X

CWVB RXO ITJ IQ JRV BZJVW.

VDICTP 2:10   *Clue: O = M*

(handwritten: VDICTP 2:10 / EXODUS)

(handwritten annotations above lines: "AND THE CHILD GREW AND SHE BROUGHT HIM UNTO / PHARAOH'S DAUGHTER AND HE BECAME HER SON AND / SHE CALLED HIS NAME MOSES AND SHE SAID BECAUSE I / DREW HIM OUT OF THE WATER")

(handwritten: EXODUS / JUDGES / EXODUS / JOSH / pharoah)

DZ GPSMY CNBKB, LYKO YK LPB ANCK MN ZKPWB,

WKGTBKI MN DK APRRKI MYK BNO NG HYPWPNY'B

IPTQYMKW; AYNNBSOQ WPMYKW MN BTGGKW

PGGRSAMSNO LSMY MYK HKNHRK NG QNI, MYPO

MN KOXNZ MYK HRKPBTWKB NG BSO GNW P

BKPBNO.

YKDWKLB 11:24–25   *Clue: A = C*

(handwritten above lines: "BY FAITH MOSES WHEN HE WAS COME TO YEARS / REFUSED TO BE CALLED THE SON OF PHARAOH'S / DAUGHTER CHOOSING RATHER TO SUFFER / AFFLICTION WITH THE PEOPLE OF GOD THAN / TO ENJOY THE PLEASURES OF SIN FOR A / SEASON")

(handwritten: HEBREWS)

BEHOLD THE EYE OF THE LORD IS UPON THEM
FDMWAI, PMD DCD WB PMD AWSI NZ XEWT PMDG

THAT FEAR HIM UPON THEM THAT HOPE IN HIS
PMKP BDKS MNG, XEWT PMDG PMKP MWED NT MNZ

MERCY
GDSLC.

EZKAG 33:18   *Clue: W = O*
PSALM

BLESSED BE THE GOD AND FATHER OF OUR LORD
AXTZZTU AT CDT IEU OPU WOCDTY EW ENY XEYU

JESUS CHRIST WHICH ACCORDING TO HIS ABUNDANT
GTZNZ KDYJZC, QDJKD OKKEYUJPI CE DJZ OANPUOPC

MERCY HATH BEGOTTEN US AGAIN UNTO A LIVELY HOPE
FTYKB DOCD ATIECCTP NZ OIOJP NPCE O XJLTXB DEVT

BY THE RESURRECTION OF JESUS CHRIST FROM THE
AB CDT YTZNYYTKCJEP EW GTZNZ KDYJZC WYEF CDT

DEAD
UTOU.

1 VTCTY 1:3   *Clue: A = B*
I PETER 1:3

XJLTXB
LIVELY

6 Lives Changed

NOW WHEN THEY SAW THE BOLDNESS OF PETER AND
MVF FKRM WKRH IPF WKR SVUOMRII VC NRWRT PMO

JOHN AND PERCEIVED THAT THEY WERE UNLEARNED
EVKM, PMO NRTJRGZRO WKPW WKRH FRTR BMURPTMRO

AND IGNORANT MEN THEY MARVELLED AND THEY
PMO GQMVTPMW LRM, WKRH LPTZRUURO; PMO WKRH

TOOK KNOWLEDGE OF THEM THAT THEY HAD BEEN
WVVY YMVFUROQR VC WKRL, WKPW WKRH KPO SRRM

WITH JESUS
FGWK ERIBI.

PJWI 4:13   *Clue: U = L*
ACTS

AND ZACCHAEUS STOOD AND SAID UNTO THE LORD
UHP EUQQSUFRB BVAAP, UHP BULP RHVA VSF NAWP:

BEHOLD LORD THE HALF OF MY GOODS I GIVE TO
CFSANP, NAWP, VSF SUNG AG XD TAAPB L TLOF VA

THE POOR AND IF I HAVE TAKEN ANY THING FROM
VSF ZAAW; UHP LG L SUOF VUIFH UHD VSLHT GWAX

ANY MAN BY FALSE ACCUSATION I RESTORE HIM
UHD XUH CD GUNBF UQQRBUVLAH, L WFBVAWF SLX

FOURFOLD AND JESUS SAID UNTO HIM THIS DAY IS
GARWGANP. UHP KFBRB BULP RHVA SLX, VSLB PUD LB

SALVATION COME TO THIS HOUSE
BUNOUVLAH QAXF VA VSLB SARBF.

NRIF 19:8–9   *Clue: O = V*
LUKE   K=J   G = S/T

                                                   B = M/N/S/T

7 Powerful Stuff

MY SOUL CLEAVETH UNTO THE DUST QUICKEN THOU ME
OS IYBE KEVUJVAP BWAY APV FBIA: RBCKDVW APYB OV

ACCORDING TO THY WORD
UKKYLFCWX AY APS NYLF.

QIUEO 119:25
PSALM

Clue: W = N

FOR THE WORD OF GOD IS QUICK AND POWERFUL AND
YPF LUW NPFA PY BPA CH GVCQZ, TEA RPNWFYVJ, TEA

SHARPER THAN AND TWO EDGED SWORD PIERCING
HUTFRWF LUTE TEO LNPWABWA HNPFA, RCWFQCEB

EVEN TO THEE DIVIDING ASUNDER OF SOUL AND
WMWE LP LUW ACMCACEB THVEAWF PY HPVJ TEA

SPIRIT AND OF THE JOINTS AND MARROW AND IS A
HRCFCL, TEA PY LUW KPCELH TEA DTFFPN, TEA CH T

DISCERNER OF THE THOUGHTS AND INTENS OF THE
ACHQWFEWF PY LUW LUPVBULH TEA CELWELH PY LUW

HEART
UWTFL.

UWXEWNH 4:12
HEBREWS

Clue: Y = F

Good Kings

AND THUS DID HEZEKIAH THROGHOUT AAA JUDAH
MCL WTVQ LYL TZXZGYMT WTAIVUTIVW MFF KVLMT,

AND WROUGHT THAT WHICH WAS GOOD AND RIGHT AND
MCL JAIVUTW WTMW JTYPT JMQ UIIL MCL AYUTW MCL

TRUTH BEFORE THE LORD HIS GOD
WAVWT SZEIAZ WTZ FIAL TYQ UIL.

2 PTAICYPFZQ 31:20   *Hezekiah*   Clue: A = R
    CHRONICLES

AND JOSIAH TOOK AWAY ALL THE ADOMINATIONS OUT
BCS WVTEBO PVVA BLBI BRR POG BKVQECBPEVCT VXP

OF ALL THE COUNRIES THAT PERTAINED TO THE
VM BRR POG YVXCPJEGT POBP FGJPBECGS PV POG

CHILDREN OF ISRAEL AND MADE ALL THAT WERE
YOERSJGC VM ETJBGR, BCS QBSG BRR POBP LGJG

PRESENT IN ISRAEL TO SERVE EVEN TO SERVE THE
FJGTGCP EC ETJBGR PV TGJZG, GZGC PV TGJZG POG

LORD THEIR GOD
RVJS POGEJ HVS.

2 YOJVCEYRGT 34:33   *Josiah*   Clue: S = D
    CHRONICLES

9 Bad Kings

BUT HE DID THAT WHICHWAS EVIL IN THE SIGHT
FWA GY RKR AGUA LGKIG LUP YBKT KQ AGY PKJGA

OF THE LORD AS DID MANASSEH HIS FATHER FOR
SD AGY TSCR, UP RKR ZUQUPPYG GKP DUAGYC: DSC

AMON SACRIFICED UNTO ALL THE CARVED IMAGES
UZSQ PUICKDKIYR WQAS UTT AGY IUCBYR KZUJYP

WHICH MANASSEH HIS FATHER HAD MADE AND
LGKIG ZUQUPPYG GKP DUAGYC GUR ZURY, UQR

SERVED THEM
PYCBYR AGYZ.

AMON

2 IGCSQKITYP 33:22
CHRONICLES

Clue: Z = M

AND AHAB THE SON OF OMRI DID EVIL IN THE
CGQ CYCF DYN PZG ZU ZWKT QTQ NBTH TG DYN

SIGHT OF THE LORD ABOVE ALL THAT WERE
PTMYD ZU DYN HZKQ CFZBN CHH DYCD RNKN

BEFORE HIM
FNUZKN YTW.

1 VTGMP 16:30
KINGS

AHAB

Clue: F = B

10 Spiritual Fruit

EVEN SO EVERY GOOD TREE BRINGETH FORTH GOOD
VLVJ YP VLVCI TPPG BCVV ZCSJTVBD KPCBD TPPG

FRUIT BUT A CORRUPT TREE BRINGETH FORTH EVIL
KCMSB; ZMB X QPCCMAB BCVV ZCSJTVBD KPCBD VLSR

FRUIT
KCMSB.

ee
FXBBDVU 7:17

MATTHEW

y = S
T

v = i
A

Clue: T = G

BUT NOW BEING MADE FREE FROM SIN AND
GAU WFY GHCWE SXNH TBHH TBFS RCW, XWN

BECOME SERVANTS TO GOD YE HAVE YOUR FRUIT
GHQFSH RHBIXWUR UF EFN, LH OXIH LFAB TBACU

UNTO HOLINESS AND THE END EVERLASTING
AWUF OFJCWHRR, XWN UOH HWN HIHBJXRUCWE

LIFE
JCTH.

BFSXWR 6:22

ROMANS

Clue: G = B

11 Simon Says

AND SIMON PETER ANSWERED AND SAID THOU ART
NVC YJKGV FHRHO NVYZHOHC NVC YNJC, RAGD NOR

THE CHRIST THE SON OF THE LIVING GOD
RAH SAOJYR, RAH YGV GQ RAH XJPJVM MGC.

MATTHEW
KNRRAHZ 16:16

Clue: V = N

PETER SAID UNTO HIM LORD WHY CANNOT I FOLLOW
OVFVA EHBT ZPFI QBJ, UIAT, KQM NHPPIF B RIUUIK

THEE NOW I WILL LAD DOWNMY LIFE FOR THY SAKE
FQVV PIK? B KBUU UHM TIKP JM UBRV RIA FQM EHWV.

JOHN
GIQP 13:37

Clue: K = W

12   *The Flood*

ANDGODSAID UNTO NOAH THE END OF ALL
MUB FAB PMGB WUCA UAMD, CDY YUB AH MNN

FLESH IS COMEBEFOREME FORTHE EARTH IS
HNYPD GP SAEY VYHALY EY; HAL CDY YMLCD GP

FILLED WITH VIOLENCE THROUGH THEM AND
HGNNYB OGCD RGANYUSY CDLAWFD CDYE; MUB,

BEHOLD I WILL DESTROY THEM WITH THE EARTH
VYDANB, G OGNN BYPCLAT CDYE OGCD CDY YMLCD.

FYUYPGP 6:13
GENESIS

Clue: H = F

AND NOAH DID ACCORDING UNTO ALL WHAT THE LORD
JBY BIJA YKY JWWIZYKBC VBNI JQQ NAJN NAD QIZY

COMMANDED HIM
WIUUJBYDY AKU.
commanded

CDBDRKR 7:5
GENESIS

Clue: N = T

13 Old Testament Miracles

AND THE LORD SAID UNTO MOSES STRETCH OUT THINE
JCA YLI STGA DJBA OCYT FTDID, DYGIYZL TOY YLBCI

HAND TOWARD HEAVEN THAT THERE MAY BE DARKNESS OVER
LJCA YTXJGA LIJEIC, YLJY YLIGI FJH WI AJGQCIDD TEIG

THE LAND OF EGYPT EVEN DARKNES WHICH MAY BE FELT
YLI SJCA TV IMHRY, IEIC AJGQCIDD XLBZL FJH WI VISY.

IUTAOD 10:21   *Clue: F = M*
EXODUS

AND IT CAME TO PASS AS THEY WERE BURYING A
BRJ QH PBZK HA TBMM, BM HDKX SKOK LIOXQRU B

MAN THAT BEHOLD THEY SPIED A BAND OF
ZBR, HDBH, LKDAGJ, HDKX MTQKJ B LBRJ AV

MEN AND THEY CAST THE MAN INTO THE SEPULCHRE
ZKR; BRJ HDKX PBMH HDK ZBR QRHA HDK MKTIGPDOK

OF ELISHA AND WHEN THE MAN WAS LET DOWN AND
AV KGQMDB: BRJ SDKR HDK ZBR SBM GKH JASR, BRJ

TOUCHED THE BONES OF ELISHA HE REVIVED AND
HAIPDKJ HDK LARKM AV KGQMDB, DK OKNQNKJ, BRJ

STOOD UP ON HIS FEET
MHAAJ IT AR DQM VKKH.

2 EQRUM 13:21   *Clue: L = B*
KINGS

14 The End of Time

AND MANY OF THEM THAT SLEEP IN THE DUST OF
LCK TLCR PE USHT USLU MBHHW FC USH KOMU PE

THE EARTH SHALL MAKE SOME TO EVERLASTING
USH HLZUS MSLBB LJLVH, MPTH UP HQHZBLMUFCA

LIFE AND SO ME TO SHAME AND EVERLASTING
BFEH, LCK MPTH UP MSLTH LCK HQHZBLMUFCA

CONTEMPT
DPCUHTWU.   A P A L E

KLCFHB 12:2
DANIEL   *Clue: T = M*

AND I SAW A NEW HEAVEN AND A NEW EARTH FOR
JOV R BJM J ONM FNJCNO JOV J ONM NJYUF: KHY

THE FIRST HEAVEN AND THE FIRST EARTH WERE
UFN KRYBU FNJCNO JOV UFN KRYBU NJYUF MNYN

PASSED AWAY AND THERE WAS NO MORE SEA
DJBBNV JMJW; JOV UFNYN MJB OH SHYN BNJ.

REVELATION
YNCNXJURHO 21:1   *Clue: M = W*

Great Stuff from the Psalms

15

~~FOR THE LORD KNOWETH THE WAY OF THE~~
SYH OWB CYHV ZKYIBOW OWB IUQ YS OWB

~~RIGHTEOUS BUT THE WAY OF THE UNGODLY~~
HPTWOBYNJ: GNO OWB IUQ YS OWB NKTYVCQ

~~SHALL PERISH~~
JWUCC ABHPJW.

~~PSALM~~ AJUCE 1:6

Clue: Q = Y

~~IT IS A GOOD THING TO GIVE THANKS UNTO THE~~
'CH CF W PLLG HOCAP HL PCZS HOWARF XAHL HOS

~~LORD AND TO SING PRAISES UNTO THY NAME O~~
YLQG, WAG HL FCAP DQWCFSF XAHL HOK AWUS, L

~~MOST HIGH TO SHEW FORTH THY LOVINGKINDNESS~~
ULFH OCPO: HL FOSN ILQHO HOK YLZCAPRCAGASFF

~~IN THE MORNING AND THY FAITHFULNESS EVERY~~
CA HOS ULQACAP, WAG HOK IWCHOIXYASFF SZSQK

~~NIGHT~~
ACPOH.

~~PSALM~~ DFWYU 92:1–2

Clue: P = G

More Great Stuff from the Psalms

THERE IS A RIVER THE STREAMS WHEREOF SHALL
SJBOB TE M OTRBO, SJB ESOBMDE QJBOBIP EJMZZ

MAKE GLAD THE CITY OF GOD THE HOLY PLACE OF THE
DMFB HZMV SJB UTSG IP HIV, SJB JIZG WZMUB IP SJB

TABERNACLES OF THE MOST HIGH
SMKBOLMUZBE IP SJB DIES JTHJ.

WEMZD 46:4
PSALM

Clue: M = A

PRAISE BE THE LORD PRAISE GOD IN HIS
GATRPB KB NSB IWAY. GATRPB EWY RC SRP

SANCTUARY PRAISE HIM IN THE FIRMAMENT OF HIS
PTCLNZTAK: GATRPB SRX RC NSB HRAXTXBCN WH SRP

POWER PRAISE HIM FOR HIS MIGHTY ACTS PRAISE
GWOBA. GATRPB SRX HWA SRP XRESNK TLNP: GATRPB

HIM ACCORDING TO HIS EXCELLENT GREATNESS
SRX TLLWAYRCE NW SRP BULBIIBCN EABTNCBPP.

GPTIX 150:1–2
PSALM

Clue: L = C

17 John the Baptist

FOR I SAY UNTO YOU AMONG THOSE THAT ARE BORN OF
IRT U ECP QKBR PRQ, CYRKL BOREJ BOCB CTJ DRTK RI

WOMEN THERE IS NOT A GREATER PROPHET THAN JOHN
FRYJK BOJTJ UE KRB C LTJCBJT ATRAOJB BOCK VROK

THE BAPTIST BUT HE THAT IS LEAST IN THE
BOJ DCABUEB: DQB OJ BOCB UE SJCEB UK BOJ

KINGDOM OF GOD IS GREATER THAN HE
XUKLMRY RI LRM UE LTJCBJT BOCK OJ.

LUKE
SQXJ 7:28   *Clue: L = G*
LUKE

FOR JOHN THE BAPTIST CAME NEITHER EATING BREAD
JFS HFIY VIO ADTVERV WDPO YOEVIOS ODVEYQ ASODL

NOR DRINKING WINE AND YE SAY HE HATH A DEVIL
YFS LSEYZEYQ MEYO; DYL UO RDU, IO IDVI D LOXEC.

THE SON OF MAN IS COME EATING AND DRINKING
VIO RFY FJ PDY ER WFPO ODVEYQ DYL LSEYZEYQ;

AND YE SAY BEHOLD A GLUTTONOUS MAN AND A
DYL UO RDU, AOIFCL D QCBVVFYFBR PDY, DYL D

WINEBIBBER A FRIEND OF PUBLICANS AND SINNERS!
MEYOAEAAOS, D JSEOYL FJ TBACEWDYR DYL REYYOSR!

LUKE
CBZO 7:33–34   *Clue: A = B*

18 · *Precious Metals*

YE SHALL NOT MAKE WITH ME GODS OF SILVER
CJ NMUHH IAP YUFJ QWPM YJ EAKN AG NWHXJO,

NEITHER SHALL YE MAKE UNTO YOU GODS OF GOLD
TJWPMJO NMUHH CJ YUFJ BTPA CAB EAKN AG EAHK.

JSAKBN 20:23   *Clue: U = A*
EXODUS

AND THE TWELVE GATES WERE TWELVE PEARLS EVERY
SBT CVJ CQJDPJ ISCJG QJMJ CQJDPJ EJSMDG: JPJMR

SEVERAL GATE WAS OF ONE PEARL AND THE STREET OF
GJPJMSD ISCJ QSG YX YBJ EJSMD: SBT CVJ GCMJJC YX

THE CITY WAS PURE GOLD AS IT WERE TRANSPARENT
CVJ LHCR QSG EFMJ IYDT, SG HC QJMJ CMSBGESMJBC

GLASS
IDSGG.

MJPJDSCHYB 21:21   *Clue: I = G*
REVELATION

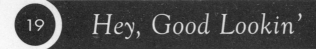

19 · Hey, Good Lookin'

BUT IN ALL ISRAEL THERE WAS NONE TO BE SO
XZJ NC MWW NHFMLW JKLFL BMH CDCL JD XL HD

MUCH PRAISED AS ABSALOM FOR HIS BEAUTY FROM
SZPK UFMNHLY MH MXHMWDS EDF KNH XLMZJV: EFDS

THE SOLE OF HIS FOOT EVEN TO THE CROWN OF HIS
JKL HDWL DE KNH EDDJ LGLC JD JKL PFDBC DE KNH

HEAD THERE WAS NO BLEMISH IN HIM
KLMY JKLFL BMH CD XWLSNHK NC KNS.

2 SAMUEL 14:25
2 HMSZLW 14:25

Clue: C = N

AND HE BROUGHT UP HADASSAH THAT IS ESTHER
DRU SL XNAFMSV FJ SDUDCCDS, VSDV HC, LCVSLN,

HIS UNCLE'S DAUGHTER FOR SHE HAD NEITHER
SHC FRZWL'C UDFMSVLN: GAN CSL SDU RLHVSLN

FATHER NOR MOTHER AND THE MAID WAS FAIR AND
GDVSLN RAN PAVSLN, DRU VSL PDHU YDC GDHN DRU

BEAUTIFUL WHOM MORDECAI WHEN HER FATHER AND
XLDFVHGFW; YSAP PANULZDH, YSLR SLN, GDVSLN DRU

MOTHER WERE DEAD TOOK FOR HIS OWN DAUGHTER
PAVSLN YLNL ULDU, VAAO GAN SHC AYR UDFMSVLN.

ESTHER 2:7
LCVSLN 2:7

Clue: G = F

20 *Prophets in General*

AND HE SAID HEAR NOW MY WORDS IF THERE BE
RXG SN URLG, SNRH XBD CF DBHGU: LY ASNHN IN

A PROPHET AMONG YOU I THE LORD WILL MAKE
R MHBMSNA RCBXP FBW, L ASN JBHG DLJJ CRON

MYSELF KNOWN UNTO HIM IN A VISION AND WILL
CFUNJY OXBDX WXAB SLC LX R TLULBX, RXG DLJJ

SPEAK UNTO HIM IN A DREAM
UMNRO WXAB SLC LX R GHNRC.

NUMBERS
XWCINHU 12:6

Clue: M = P

BUT THE PROPHET WHICH SHALL PRESUME TO SPEAK A
QWC CJY LDSLJYC, NJUAJ TJKEE LDYTWGY CS TLYKM K

WORD IN MY NAME WHICH I HAVE NOT COMMANDED HIM
NSDR UI GX IKGY, NJUAJ U JKOY ISC ASGGKIRYR JUG

TO SPEAK OR THAT SHALL SPEAK IN THE NAME OF OTHER
CS TLYKM, SD CJKC TJKEE TLYKM UI CJY IKGY SH SCJYD

GODS EVEN THAT PROPHET SHALL DIE
VSRT, YOYI CJKC LDSLJYC TJKEE RUY.

DEUTERONOMY
RYWCYDSISGX 18:20

Clue: G = M

21 *Prophets in Specific*

AND THEY TOLD THE KING SAYING BEHOLD NATHAN
SOV PLYD PZGV PLY MWOI, HSDWOI, NYLZGV OSPLSO

THE PROPHET AND WHEN HE WAS COME IN BEFORE THE
PLY AFZALYP. SOV JLYO LY JSH UZBY WO NYRZFY PLY

KING HE BOWED HIMSELF BEFORE THE KING WITH
MWOI, LY NZJYV LWBHYGR NYRZFY PLY MWOI JWPL

HIS FACE TO THE GROUND
LWH RSUY PZ PLY IFZXOV.

KINGS
1 MWOIH 1:23   *Clue: I = G*

HOW LONG HALT YE BETWEEN TWO OPINIONS IF THE
YCI FCWX YUFV QL OLVILLW VIC CNSWSCWG? ST VYL

LORD BE GOD FOLLOW HIM BUT IF BAAL THEN FOLLOW HIM
FCZP OL XCP, TCFFCI YSA: OJV ST OUUF, VYLW TCFFCI YSA.

AND THE PEOPLE ANSWERED HIM NOT A WORD THEN SAID
UWP VYL NLCNFL UWGILZLP YSA WCV U ICZP. VYLW GUSP

ELIJAH UNTO THE PEOPLE I EVEN I ONLY REMAIN A
LFSMUY JWVC VYL NLCNFL, S, LHLW S CWFQ, ZLAUSW U

PROPHET OF THE LORD BUT BAAL'S PROPHETS ARE FOUR
NZCNYLV CT VYL FCZP; OJV OUUF'G NZCNYLVG UZL TCJZ

HUNDRED AND FIFTY MEN
YJWPZLP UWP TSTVQ ALW.

KINGS
1 ESWXG 18:21–22   *Clue: O = B*

22 More Prophets in Specific

IN THOSE DAYS WAS HEZEKIAH SICK UNTO DEATH AND
SJ DFGRK OXQR IXR FKMKNSXF RSBN EJDG OKXDF. XJO

ISAIAH THE PROPHET THE SON OF AMOZ CAME UNTO
SRXSXF DFK HLGHFKD DFK RGJ GV XUGM BXUK EJDG

HIM AND SAID UNTO HIM THUS SAITH THE LORD SET
FSU, XJO RXSO EJDG FSU, DFER RXSDF DFK CGLO, RKD

THINE HOUSE IN ORDER FOR THOU SHALT DIE AND NOT
DFSJK FGERK SJ GLOKL: VGL DFGE RFXCD OSK, XJO JGD

LIVE
CSAK.

SRXSXF 38:1
ISAIAH

Clue: E = U

EVEN THE PROPHET JEREMIAH SAID AMEN THE
AIAD SBA HCTHBAS MACAQWNB RNWP, NQAD: SBA

LORD DO SO THE LORD PERFORM THY WORDS WHICH
YTCP PT RT: SBA YTCP HACKTCQ SBU XTCPR XBWZB

THOU HAST PROPHESIED TO BRING AGAIN THE
SBTV BNRS HCTHBARWAP, ST ECWDL NLNWD SBA

VESSELS OF THE LORD'S HOUSE AND ALL THAT IS
IARRAYR TK SBA YTCP'R BTVRA, NDP NYY SBNS WR

CARRIED AWAY CAPTIVE FROM BABYLON INTO
ZNCCWAP NXNU ZNHSWIA, KCTQ ENEUYTD WDST

THIS PLACE
SBWR HYNZA.

MACAQWNB 28:6
JEREMIAH

Clue: E = B

Key Ideas of the New Testament

23

NOW THERE ARE DIVERSITES OF GIFTS BUT THE
TNO IDRMR SMR GPFRMUPIPRU NA LPAIU, HQI IDR

SAME SPIRIT AND THERE ARE DIFFERNCES OF
USZR UBPMPI. STG IDRMR SMR GPAARMRTKRU NA

ADMINISTRATIONS BUT THE SAME LORD AND THERE
SGZPTPUIMSIPNTU, HQI IDR USZR VNMG. STG IDRMR

ARE DIVERSITIES OF OPERATIONS BUT IT IS THE
SMR GPFRMUPIPRU NA NBRMSIPNTU, HQI PI PU IDR

SAME GOD WHICH WORKETH ALL IN ALL
USZR LNG ODPKD ONMERID SVV PT SVV.

CORINTHIANS
1 KNMPTIDPSTU 12:4–6   *Clue: O = W*

AND EVERY PRIEST STANDETH DAILY
OCE HQHWM VWNHPK PKOCEHKL EONXM

MINISTERING AND OFFERING OFTENTIMES THE
FNCNPKHWNCA OCE YBBHWNCA YBKHCKNFHP KLH

SAME SACRIFICES WHICH CAN NEVER TAKE
POFH POSWNBNSHP, ULNSL SOC CHQHW KOIH

AWAY SINS BUT THIS MAN AFTER HE HAD
OUOM PNCP: DJK KLNP FOC, OBKHW LH LOE

OFFERED ONE SACRIFICE FOR SINS FOR EVER
YBBHWHE YCH POSWNBNSH BYW PNCP BYW HQHW,

SAT DOWN ON THE RIGHT HAND OF GOD
POK EYUC YC KLH WNALK LOCE YB AYE.

HEBREWS
LHDWHUP 10:11–12   *Clue: A = G*

24 Cleanliness Is Next to Godliness

HE SHALL THEREFORE BURN THAT GARMENT
NS FNWEE KNSVSPRVS JAVG KNWK HWVOSGK,

WHETHER WARP OR WOOF IN WOOLLEN OR IN LINEN
CNSKNSV CWVZ RV CRRP, LG CRREESG RV LG ELGSG,

OR ANYTHING OF SKIN WHEREIN THE PLAGUE IS
RV WGQ KNLGH RP FBLG, CNSVSLG KNS ZEWHAS LF:

FOR IT IS A FRETTING LEPROSY IT SHALL BE BURNT
PRV LK LF W PVSKKLGH ESZVRFQ; LK FNWEE JS JAVGK

IN THE FIRE
LG KNS PLVS.

ESYLKLXAF 13:52   *Clue: E – L*
LEVITICUS

AND THE LEPER IN WHO THE PLAGUE IS HIS
KCE VNS DSJSL OC BNTI VNS JDKYRS OQ, NOQ

CLOTHES SHALL BE RENT AND HIS HEAD BARE AND
HDTVNSQ QNKDD FS LSCV, KCE NOQ NSKE FKLS, KCE

HE SHALL PUT A COVERING UPON HIS UPPER LIP
NS QNKDD JRV K HTGSLOCY RJTC NOQ RJJSL DOJ,

AND SHALL CRY UNCLEAN UNCLEAN ALL THE DAYS
KCE QNKDD HLU, RCHDSKC, RCHDSKC. KDD VNS EKUQ

WHEREIN THE PLAGUE SHALL BE IN H IM HE SHALL
BNSLSOC VNS JDKYRS QNKDD FS OC NOI NS QNKDD

BE DEFILED HE IS UNCLEAN HE SHALL DWELL ALONE
FS ESXODSE; NS OQ RCHDSKC: NS QNKDD EBSDD KDTCS.

LEVITICUS
DSGOVOHRQ 13:45–46   *Clue: R = U*

25 Verses Worth Memorizing

FOR GOD COMMENDETH HIS LOVE TOWARD US IN THAT
YDI QWG UWNNJLGJIF FKA HWZJ IWPRBG DA, KL IFRI,

WHILE WE WERE YET SINNERS CHRIST DIED FOR US
PFKHJ PJ PJBJ CJI AKLIJBA, UFBKAI GKJG XWB DA.

BWNRLA 5:8
ROMANS

Clue: U = C

BE NOT DECEIVED GOD IS NOT MOCKED FOR
WB MHK CBZBLXBC; YHC LE MHK VHZDBC: OHU

WHATSOEVER A MAN SOWETH THAT SHALL HE ALSO REAP
QJFKEHBXBU F VFM EHQBKJ, KJFK EJFPP JB FPEH UBFR.

FOR HE THAT SOWETH TO HIS FLESH SHALL OF THE
OHU JB KJFK EHQBKJ KH JLE OPBEJ EJFPP HO KJB

FLESH REAP CORRUPTION BUT HE THAT SOWETH TO THE
OPBEJ UBFR ZHUUIRKLHM; WIK JB KJFK EHQBKJ KH KJB

SPIRIT SHALL OF THE SPIRIT REAP LIFE EVERLASTING
ERLULK EJFPP HO KJB ERLULK UBFR PLOB BXBUPFEKLMY.

GALATIANS
YFPFKLFME 6:7–8

Clue: R = P

Attributes of God

NOW UNTO THE KING ETERNAL IMMORTAL
PUO TPHU HJG DWPR GHGMPIE, WLLUMHIE,

INVISIBLE THE ONLY WISE GOD BE HONOUR AND
WPSWAWCEG, HJG UPEN OWAG RUK, CG JUPUTM IPK

GLORY FOR EVER AND EVER AMEN
REUMN ZUM GSGM IPK GSGM. ILGP.

T IMOTHY
1 HWLUHJN 1:17

Clue: P = N

THEN CAME THE WORD OF THE LORD UNTO JEREMIAH
JIPL GUOP JIP CWST WK JIP DWST XLJW YPSPOFUI,

SAYING BEHOLD I AM THE LORD THE GOD OF ALL
EUNFLB, HPIWDT, F UO JIP DWST, JIP BWT WK UDD

FLESH IS THERE ANY THING TOO HARD FOR ME
KDPEI: FE JIPSP ULN JIFLB JWW IUST KWS OP?

JEREMIAH
YPSPOFUI 32:26–27

Clue: O = M

27   *Real Smarts*

THE FEAR OF THE LORD IS THE BEGINNING OF WISDOM
BDY LYJX SL BDY USXF VA BDY TYWVHHVHW SL PVAFSG:

A GOOD UNDERSTANDING HAVE ALL THEY THAT DO HIS
J WSSF CHFYXABJHFVHW DJNY JUU BDYR BDJB FS DVA

COMMANDMENTS HIS PRAISE ENDURETH FOR EVER
QSGGJHFGYHBA: DVA TXJVAY YHFCXYBD LSX YNYX.

PSALM
TAJUG 111:10   *Clue: W = G*

WISDOM IS THE PRINCIPAL THING THEREFORE
OJHMSR JH EVY FWJBPJFCU EVJBA; EVYWYNSWY

GET WISDOM AND WITH ALL THY GETTING GET
AYE OJHMSR: CBM OJEV CUU EVD AYEEJBA AYE

UNDERSTANDING
ZBMYWHECBMJBA.

PROVERBS
FWSKYWXH 4:7   *Clue: J = I*

28 — Jonah's Story

ARISE GO TO NINEVEH THAT GREAT CITY AND CRY
KIHNP, CV FV OHOPEPD, FDKF CIPKF SHFM, KOZ SIM

AGAINST IT FOR THEIR WICKEDNESS IS COME
KCKHONF HF; BVI FDPHI UHSAPZOPNN HN SVQP

UP BEFORE ME BUT JONAH ROSE UP TO FLEE UNTO
LW RPBVIP QP. RLF XVOKD IVNP LW FV BTPP LOFV

TARSHISH FROM THE PRESENCE OF THE LORD AND
FKINDHND BIVQ FDP WIPNPOSP VB FDP TVIZ, KOZ

WENT DOWN TO JOPPA
UPOF ZVUO FV XVWWK.

JONAH
XVOKD 1:2–3

Clue: S = C

I CRIED BY REASON OF MINE AFFLICTION UNTO THE
A SGAYN CZ GYFDRJ RK LAJY FKKTASUARJ BJUR UEY

LORD AND HE HEARD ME OUT OF THE BELLY OF HELL
TRGN, FJN EY EYFGN LY; RBU RK UEY CYTTZ RK EYTT

CRIED I AND THOU HEARDEST MY VOICE FOR THOU
SGAYN A, FJN UERB EYFGNYDU LZ ORASY. KRG UERB

HADST CAST ME INTO THE DEEP IN THE MIDST OF
EFNDU SFDU LY AJUR UEY NYYM, AJ UEY LANDU RK

THE SEAS AND THE FLOODS COMPASSED ME ABOUT
UEY DYFD; FJN UEY KTRRND SRLMFDDYN LY FCRBU.

JONAH
XRJFE 2:2–3

Clue: C = B

29 Lamentable

HOW HATH THE LORD COVERED THE DAUGHTER OF ZION WITH
IZC IEBI BIJ MZKS OZUJKJS BIJ SENRIBJK ZD GQZL CQBI

A CLOUD IN HIS ANGER AND CAST DOWN FROM HEAVEN
E OMZNS QL IQX ELRJK, ELS OEXB SZCL DKZF IJEUJL

UNTO THE EARTH THE BEAUTY OF ISRAEL AND REMEMERED
NLBZ BIJ JEKBI BIJ AJENBW ZD QXKEJM, ELS KJFFAJKJS
REMEMBERED

NOT HIS FOOTSTOOL IN THE DAY OF HIS ANGER!
LZB IQX DZZBXBZZM QL BIJ SEW ZD IQX ELRJK!

MEFJLBEBQZLX 2:1
LAMENTATIONS

Clue: M = L

FOR THE LORD WILL NOT CAST OFF FOR EVER
DHA SXC KHAR ENKK PHS VUIS HDD DHA CGCA:

BUT THOUGH HE CAUSE GRIEF YET WILL HE HAVE
LOS SXHOBX XC VUOIC BANCD, JCS ENKK XC XUGC

COMPASSION ACCORDING TO THE MULTITUDE OF HIS
VHZFUIINHP UVVHARNPB SH SXC ZOKSNSORC HD XNI

MERCIES
ZCAVNCI.

KUZCPSUSNHPJ 3:31–32
LAMENTATIONS

Clue: U = A

30   *Parables of Jesus*

AND HE SPAKE A PARABLE UNTO THEM CAN THE
JSH MW DFJQW J FJCJLRW OSAP AMWE, NJS AMW

BLIND LEAD THE BLIND SHALL THEY NOT BOTH
LRYSH RWJH AMW LRYSH? DMJRR AMWT SPA LPAM

FALL INTO THE DITCH
VJRR YSAP AMW HYANM?

~~JOHN~~
ROQW 6:39
~~MARK~~
LUKE

Clue: L = B

THE KINGDOM OF HEAVEN IS LIKE TO A GRAIN OF
ORN HEFDLUS UW RNIKNF EV PEHN OU I DTIEF UW

MUSTARD SEED WHEN A MAN TOOK AND SOWED IN HIS
SCVOITL VNNL, ZREJR I SIF OUUH, IFL VUZNL EF REV

FIELD WHICH INDEED IS THE LEAST OF ALL SEEDS
WENPL: ZREJR EFLNNL EV ORN PNIVO UW IPP VNNLV:

BUT WHEN IT IS GROWN IT IS THE GREATEST
MCO ZRNF EO EV DTUZF, EO EV ORN DTNIONVO

AMONG HERBS AND BECOMETH A TREE SO THAT THE
ISUFD RNTMV, IFL MNJUSNOR I OTNN, VU ORIO ORN

BIRDS OF THE AIR COME AND LODGE IN THE BRANCHES
METLV UW ORN IET JUSN IFL PULDN EF ORN MTIFJRNV

THEREOF
ORNTNUW.

MATTHEW
SIOORNZ 13:31–32

Clue: C = U

31 More Parables of Jesus

ANOTHER PARABLE SPAKE HE UNTO THEM THE
RFMGUVA ZRARJYV WZRBV UV CFGM GUVI; GUV

KINGDOM OF HEAVEN IS LIKE UNTO LEAVEN WHICH A
BLFHTMI ME UVROVF LW YLBV CFGM YVROVF, QULDU R

WOMAN TOOK AND HID IN THREE MEASURES OF MEAL
QMIRF GMMB, RFT ULT LF GUAVV IVRWCAVW ME IVRY,

TILL THE WHOLE WAS LEAVENED
GLYY GUV QUMYV QRW YVROVFVT.

MATTHEW
IRGGUVQ 13:33   *Clue: R = A*

NOW LEARN A PARABLE OF THE FIG TREE WHEN
WPQ MDYEW Y LYEYAMD PT OID TCJ OEDD; QIDW

HIS BRANCH IS YET TENDER AND PUTTETH
ICX AEYWBI CX RDO ODWGDE, YWG LZOODOI

FORTH LEAVES YE KNOW THAT SUMMER IS NIGH SO
TPEOI MDYSDX, RD VWPQ OIYO XZHHDE CX WCJI: XP

LIKEWISE YE WHEN YE SHALL SEE ALL THESE
MCVDQCXD RD, QIDW RD XIYMM XDD YMM OIDXD

THINGS KNOW THAT IT IS NEAR EVEN AT THE
OICWJX, VWPQ OIYO CO CX WDYE, DSDW YO OID

DOORS
GPPEX.

MATTHEW
HYOOIDQ 24:32–33   *Clue: M = L*

32 *Jewelry in the Bible*

AND THEY CAME BOTH MEN AND WOMEN AS
BAP MCSU IBGS, VHMC GSA BAP YHGSA, BN

MANY AS WERE WILLING HEARTED AND BROUGHT
GBAU BN YSTS YEJJEAO CSBTMSP, BAP VTHXOCM

BRACELETS AND EARRINGS AND RINGS AND TABLETS
VTBISJSMN, BAP SBTTEAON, BAP TEAON, BAP MBVJSMN,

ALL JEWELS OF GOLD AND EVERY MAN THAT OFFERED
BJJ FSYSJN HL OHJP: BAP SKSTU GBA MCBM HLLSTSP

OFFERED AN OFFERING OF GOLD UNTO THE LORD
HLLSTSP BA HLLSTEAO HL OHJP XAMH MCS JHTP.

EXODUS
SZHPXN 35:22

Clue: Y = W

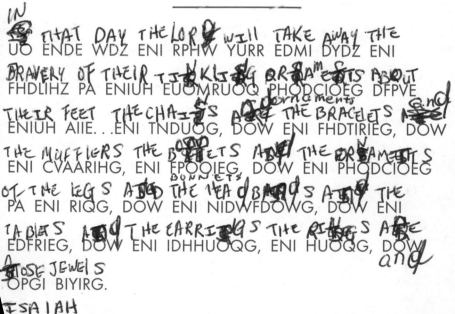

IN
THAT DAY THE LORD WILL TAKE AWAY THE
UO ENDE WDZ ENI RPHW YURR EDMI DYDZ ENI

BRAVERY OF THEIR TINKLING ORNAMENTS ABOUT
FHDLIHZ PA ENIUH EUOMRUOQ PHODCIOEG DFPVE

THEIR FEET THE CHAINS AND THE BRACELETS and
ENIUH AIIE...ENI TNDUOG, DOW ENI FHDTIRIEG, DOW

THE MUFFLERS THE BONNETS AND THE ORNAMENTS
ENI CVAARIHG, ENI FPOOIEG, DOW ENI PHODCIOEG

OF THE LEGS AND THE HEADBANDS AND THE
PA ENI RIQG, DOW ENI NIDWFDOWG, DOW ENI

TABLETS AND THE EARRINGS THE RINGS AND
EDFRIEG, DOW ENI IDHHUOQG, ENI HUOQG, DOW

AND
THOSE JEWELS
OPGI BIYIRG.

ISAIAH
UGDUDN 3:18–21

Clue: F = B

33 — Old Folks

AND LAMECH LIVED AFTER HE BEGAT NOAH FIVE
LWC KLGDPB KVJDC LAQDE BD XDILQ WNLB AVJD

HUNDRED NINETY AND FVE YEARS AND BEGAT
BZWCEDC WVWDQU LWC AVJD UDLEM, LWC XDILQ

SONS AND DAUGHTERS AND ALL THE DAYS OF
MNWM LWC CLZIBQDEM: LWC LKK QBD CLUM NA

LAMECH WERE SEVEN HUNDRED SEVENTY AND
KLGDPB ODED MDJDW BZWCEDC MDJDWQU LWC

SEVEN YEARS AND HE DIED
MDJDW UDLEM: LWC BD CVDC.

IDWDMVM 5:30–31   *Clue: K = L*
GENESIS

AND METHUSELAH LIVED AN HUNDRED EIGHTY AND
GLA ICBEHFCPGE PNSCA GL EHLAOCA CNWEBK GLA

SEVEN YEARS AND BEGAT LAMECH AND METHUSELAH
FCSCL KCGOF, GLA TCWGB PGICXE. GLA ICBEHFCPGE

LIVED AFTER HE BEGAT LAMECH SEVEN HUNDRED
PNSCA GQBCO EC TCWGB PGICXE FCSCL EHLAOCA

EIGHTY AND TWO YEARS AND BEGAT SONS AND
CNWEBK GLA BDV KCGOF, GLA TCWGB FVLF GLA

DAUGHTERS AND ALL THE DAYS OF METHUSELAH
AGHWEBCOF: GLA GPP BEC AGKF VQ ICBEHFCPGE

WERE NINE HUNDRED SIXTY AND NINE YEARS AND
DCOC LNLC EHLAOCA FNZBK GLA LNLC KCGOF: GLA

HE DIED
EC ANCA.

GENESIS
WCLCFNF 5:25–27   *Clue: N =*

34) *Theology of Romans, Part 1*

THE~~REFORE~~ BY THE deeds OF THE LAW THERE
COKDKPBDK JA COK LKKLZ BP COK URX COKDK

SHALL NO FLESH BE JUSTIFIED IN HIS SIGHT
ZORUU VB PUKZO JK YTZCWPWKL WV OWZ ZWHOC:

FOR BY THE ~~AND~~ IS THE KNOWLEDGE OF SIN
PBD JA COK URX WZ COK QVBXUKLHK BP ZWV.
        LAW

ROMANS
DBERVZ 3:20

Clue: B = O

FOR THE INVISIBLE THINGS OF HIM FROM THE CREATION
EBP YIJ SWZSVSQCJ YISWFV BE ISO EPBO YIJ LPJUYSBW

OF THE WORLD ARE CLEARLY SEEN, BEING UNDERSTOOD
BE YIJ DBPCR UPJ LCJUPCK VJJW, QJSWF MWRJPVYBBR

BY THE THINGS THAT ARE MADE EVEN HIS ETERNAL
QK YIJ YISWFV YIUY UPJ OURJ, JZJW ISV YYJPWUC

POWER AND GODHEAD SO THAT THEY ARE WITHOUT EXCUSE
TBDJP UWR FBRIJUR; VB YIUY YIJK UPJ DSYIBMY JNLMVJ:

BECAUSE THAT WHEN THEY KNEW GOD THEY GLORIFIED HIM
QJLUMVJ YIUY, DIJW YIJK XWJD FBR, YIJK FCBPSESJR ISO

NOT AS GOD NEITHER WERE THANKFUL BUT BECAME
WBY UV FBR, WJSYIJP DJPJ YIUWXEMC; QMY QJLUOJ

VAIN IN THEIR IMAGINATIONS
ZUSW SW YIJSP SOUFSWUYSBWV.

ROMANS
PBOUWV 1:20—21

Clue: S = I

FOR IF WHEN WE WERE ENEMIES WE WERE RECONCILED
CEP TC, ONJB OJ OJPJ JBJYTJK, OJ OJPJ PJWEBWTSJI

TO GOD BY THE DEATH OF HIS SON MUCH MORE BEING
QE UEI ZH QNJ IJVQN EC NTK KEB, YXWN YEPJ, ZJTBU

RECONCILED WE SHALL BE SAVED BY HIS LIFE
PJWEBWTSJI, OJ KNVSS ZJ KVLJI ZH NTK STCJ.

ROMANS
PEYVBK 5:10

Clue: C = F

THERE IS THEREFOR E NOW NO CONDEMNATION TO THEM
FLBWB HC FLBWBGJWB RJD RJ NJRZBQROFHJR FJ FLBQ

WHICH ARE IN CHRIST JESUS WHO WALL NOT AFTER
DLHNL OWB HR NLWHCF ABCYC, DLJ DOIT RJF OGFBW

THE FLESH BUT AFTER THE SPIRIT FOR THE LAW OF
FLB GIBCL, MYF OGFBW FLB CUHWHF. GJW FLB IOD JG

THE SPIRIT OF LIFE IN CHRIST JESUS HATH MADE
FLB CUHWHF JG IHGB HR NLWHCF ABCYC LOFL QOZB

ME FREE FROM THE LAW OF SIN AND DEATH
QB GWBB GWJQ FLB IOD JG CHR ORZ ZBOFL.

ROMANS
WJQORC 8:1–2

Clue: Z = D

36 *Marital Mismatch*

NOW THE NAME OF THE MAN WAS NABAL AND THE NAME
IRD VPJ IWGJ RN VPJ GWI DWY IWCWE; WIS VPJ IWGJ

OF HIS WIFE ABIGAIL AND SHE WAS A WOMAN
RN PTY DTNJ WCTXWTE: WIS YPJ DWY W DRGWI

OF GOOD UNDERSTANDING AND OF A BEAUTIFUL
RN XRRS AISJZYVWISTIX, WIS RN W CJWAVTNAE

COUNTENANCE BUT THE MAN WAS CHURLISH AND EVIL IN
FRAIVJIWIFJ: CAV VPJ GWI DWY FPAZETYP WIS JBTE TI

HIS DOINGS AND HE WAS OF THE HOUSE OF CALEB
PTY SRTIXY; WIS PJ DWY RN VPJ PRAYJ RN FWEJC.

SAMUEL
1 YWGAJE 25:3

Clue: P = H

THEN HIS FATHER AND HIS MOTHER SAID UNTO HIM IS
CALP AFD SJCALH JPZ AFD ERCALH DJFZ BPCR AFE, FD

THERE N ER A WOMAN AMONG THE DAUGHTERS OF THY
CALHL PLGLH J IREJP JERPV CAL ZJBVACLHD RS CAQ

BRETHREN OR AMONG ALL MY PEOPLE THAT THO GEST
OHLCAHLP, RH JERPV JXX EQ MLRMXL, CAJC CARB VRLDC

TO T E   E OF THE UN R UM SE   HLST E
CR CJYL J IFSL RS CAL BPWFHWBEWFDLZ MAFXFDCFPLD?

AND SAMSON SAID UNTO HIS FATHER GET HER FOR ME
JPZ DJEDRP DJFZ BPCR AFD SJCALH, VLC ALH SRH EL;

FOR SHE L SETH ME ELL
SRH DAL MXLJDLCA EL ILXX.

JUDGES
TBZVLD 14:3

Clue: S = F

TH EN ENTERED SATAN INTO JUDAS SURNAMED ISCAR IOT
LWUA UALUOUI VFLFA CALJ MPIFV VPOAFHUI CVBFOCJL,

BEING OF THE NUMBER OF TH E TWELVE AND HE
QUCAD JG LWU APHQUO JG LWU LTURYU. FAI WU

WENT HIS WAY AND COMMUNED WITH THE CHIEF
TUAL WCV TFK, FAI BJHHPAUI TCLW LWU BWCUG

PRIESTS AND CAPTAINS HOW HE MIGHT BETRAY HIM
EOCUVLV FAI BFELFCAV, WJT WU HCDWL QULOFK WCH

UNTO THEM
PALJ LWUH.

RPSU 22:3–4
LUKE

Clue: V = S

———————————

SAYING I HAVE SINNED IN THAT I HAVE BETRAYED
MPBCOR, C SPZY MCOOYH CO ASPA C SPZY VYAIPBYH

THE INNOCENT BLOOD AND THEY SAID WHAT IS
ASY COONGYOA VUNNH. POH ASYB MPCH, LSPA CM

THAT TO US SEE THOU TO THAT AND HE CAST
ASPA AN EM? MYY ASNE AN ASPA. POH SY GPMA

DOWN THE PIECES OF SILVER IN THE TEMPLE
HNLO ASY WCYGYM NX MCUZYI CO ASY AYDWUY,

AND DEPARTED AND WENT AND HANGED HIMSELF
POH HYWPIAYH, POH LYOA POH SPORYH SCDMYUX.

DPAASYL 27:4–5
MATTHEW

Clue: G = C

38 Thoughts for Philemon

C UERV GEDK IJCNNKO CN ICNG ACOK WIO GEOP, C
I PAUL HAVE WRITTEN IT WITH MINE OWN HAND I

ICVV JKUEZ CN: EVTKCN C PW OWN YEZ NW NGKK
WILL REPAY IT ALBEIT I DO NOT SAY TO THEE

GWI NGWR WIKYN RONW AK KDKO NGCOK WIO
HOW THOU OWEST UN TO ME EVEN THINE OWN

YKVB TKYCPKY.
SELF BESIDES

UGCVKAWO 1:19
PHILEMON

Clue: Y = S

K OVRGL FE UTH, FRLKGU FYGOKTG TP OVYY RIAREN
I THANK MY GOD MAKING MENTION OF THEE ALWAYS

KG FE XWREYWN, VYRWKGU TP OVE ITCY RGH PRKOV,
IN MY PRAYERS HEARING OF THY LOVE AND FAITH

AVKMV OVTD VRNO OTARWH OVY ITWH BYNDN, RGH
WHICH THOU HAST TOWARD THE LORD JESUS AND

OTARWH RII NRKGON; OVRO OVY MTFFDGKMROKTG
TOWARD ALL SAINTS THAT THE COMMUNICATION

TP OVE PRKOV FRE QYMTFY YPPYMORRI QE OVY
OF THY FAITH MAY BECOME EFFECTUAL BY THE

RMLGTAIYHUKGU TP YCYWE UTTH OVKGU AVKMV KN
ACKNOWLEDGING OF EVERY GOOD THING WHICH IS

KG ETD KG MVWKNO BYNDN.
IN YOU IN CHRIST JESUS

XVKIYFTG 1:4–6
PHILEMON

Clue: A = W

39 Goats in the Bible

or if his sin which he hath commit came to his
JN FA RFY YFH, CRFBR RL RWMR YFHHLE, BJVL MJ RFY

knowledge then he shall bring his offering a
GHJCILESL: MRLH RL YRWII ONFHS RFY JAALNFHS, W

kid of the goats a female without blemish for
GFE JA MRL SJWMY, W ALVWIL CFMRJPM OILVFYR, AJN

his sin which he hath commit
RFY YFH CRFBR RL RWMR YFHHLE.

Leviticus
ILXFMFBPY 4:28

Clue: M = T

Then saul took three thousand chosen men all of
INSR MOKJ ILLQ INFSS INLKMORC WNLMSR TSR LKI LZ

the israel and went to seek david and his men
OJJ VMFOSJ, ORC BSRI IL MSSQ COEVC ORC NVM TSR

from the rocks of the wild goats
KXLR INS FLWQM LZ INS BVJC PLOIM.

Samuel
1 MOTKSJ 24:2

Clue: C = D

40 Days of Creation

AND GOD SAID LET THERE BE LIGHTS IN THE
UIK OGK MUWK, NTH HPTLT RT NWOPHM WI HPT

FIRMAMENT OF THE HEAVEN TO DIVIDE THE DAY FROM
BWLEUETIH GB HPT PTUZTI HG KWZWKT HPT KUQ BLGE

THE NIGHT AND LET THEM BE FOR SIGNS AND FOR
HPT IWOPH; UIK NTH HPTE RT BGL MWOIM, UIK BGL

SEASON AND FOR DAYS AND YEARS AND LET THEM
MTUMGIM, UIK BGL KUQM, UIK QTULM: UIK NTH HPTE

BE FOR LIGHTS IN THE FIRMAMENT OF THE HEAVEN TO
RT BGL NWOPHM WI HPT BWLEUETIH GB HPT PTUZTI HG

GIVE LIGHT UPON THE EARTH AND IT WAS SO
OWZT NWOPH VFGI HPT TULHP: UIK WH SUM MG.

OTITMWM 1:14–15   *Clue: B = F*
GENESIS

_____

AND GOD CREATED GREAT WHALES AND EVERY LIVING
TRP LSP HVOTDOP LVOTD ZXTBOJ, TRP ONOVC BANARL

CREATURE THAT MOVETH WHICH THE WATERS BROUGHT
HVOTDMVO DXTD YSNODX, ZXAHX DXO ZTDOVJ IVSMLXD

FORTH ABUNDANLY AFTER THEIR KIND AND EVERY
WSVDX TIMRPTRDBC, TWDOV DXOAV UARP, TRP ONOVC

WINGED FOWL AFTER HIS KIND AND GOD SAW THAT IT
ZARLOP WSZB TWDOV XAJ UARP: TRP LSP JTZ DXTD AD

WAS GOOD AND GOD BLESSED THEM SAYING BE FRUITFUL
ZTJ LSSP. TRP LSP IBOJJOP DXOY, JTCARL, IO WVMADWMB,

AND MULTIPLY
TRP YMBDAFBC.

LOROJAJ 1:21–22   *Clue: L = G*
GENESIS

41 *Cities in Acts*

(handwritten solution above line:) AND A CERTAIN WOMAN NAMED LYDIA A SELLER
NGU N DFOCNJG SBING GNIFU RXUJN, N TFRRFO

(handwritten:) OF PURPLE OF THE CITY OF THYATIRA WHICH
BE LPOLRF, BE CWF DJCX BE CWXNCJON, SWJDW

(handwritten:) WORSHIPPED GOD HEARD US WHOSE HEART THE
SBOTWJLLFU ABU, WFNOU PT: SWBTF WFNOC CWF

(handwritten:) LORD OPENED TH AT SHE ATTENDED UNTO THE
RBOU BLFGFU, CWNC TWF NCCFGUFU PGCB CWF

(handwritten:) THINGS WHICH WERE SPOKEN OF PAUL
CWJGAT SWJDW SFOF TLBVFG BE LNPR.

NDCT 16:14
ACTS

Clue: U = D

(handwritten:) A THE BETHREA E ATE Y SE T AWAY
FPQ VTW SLWVTLWP JCCWQJFVWIX NWPV FEFX

(handwritten:) A A S AS BY A H T ATO BEREA WHO C A
HFOI FPQ NJIFN SX PJKTV OPVD SWLWF: ETD RDCJPK

(handwritten:) TH THE R WE T ATO THE S A B E O THE NEWS
VTJVTWL EWPV JPVD VTW NXPFKDKOW DZ VTW GWEN.

(handwritten:) ROME
FRVN 17:10
ACTS

Clue: E = W

42 Old Testament Mothers

WHEREFORE IT CAME TO PASS, WHEN THE TIME WAS
CQLSLMNSL BJ TGFL JN RGAA, CQLD JQL JBFL CGA

COME ABOUT AFTER HANNAH HAD CONCEIVED THAT
TNFL GONYJ GMJLS QGDDGQ QGI TNDTLBELI, JQGJ

SHE BARE A SON AND CALLED HIS NAME SAMUEL
AQL OGSL G AND, GDI TGKKLI QBA DGFL AGFYLK,

SAYING BECAUSE I HAVE ASKED HIM OF THE LORD
AGUBDP, OLTGYAL B QGEL GAWLI QBF NM JQL KNSI.

1 AGFYLK 1:20   *Clue: O = B*
  SAMUEL

AND HAGAR BARE ABRAM A SON AND ABRAM CALLED HIS
EHZ KEOEP XEPA EXPEV E RDH: EHZ EXPEV JEYYAZ KGR

SON'S NAME WHICH HAGAR BARE ISHMAEL
RDH'R HEVA, UKGJK KEOEP XEPA, GRKVEAY.

OAHARGR 16:15   *Clue: V = M*
GENESIS

More Old Testament Mothers

43

FOR SARAH CONCEIVED AND BARE ABRAHAM A SON IN
QGA BSASI JGLJURDUP, SLP WSAU SWASISC S BGL RL

HIS OLD AGE AT THE SET TIME OF WHICH GOD HAD
IRB GEP SNU, SM MIU BUM MRCU GQ FIRJI NGP ISP

SPOKEN TO HIM   WHICH
BHGVUL MG IRC.

NULUBRB 21:2
GENESIS

Clue: I = H

SO BOAZ TOOK RUTH AND SHE WAS HIS WIFE AND
GL HLTQ KLLX NCKY, TRI GYO UTG YWG UWSO: TRI

WHEN HE WENT IN UNTO HER THE LORD GAVE HER
UYOR YO UORK WR CRKL YON, KYO ZLNI PTJO YON

CONCEPTION AND SHE BARE A SON
ALRAODKWLR, TRI GYO HTNO T GLR.

NCKY 4:13
RUTH

Clue: W = I

44 Jesus' Words to the Churches

SO THEN BECAUSE THOU ART LUKEWARM AND
WN QRDI ZDHPMWD QRNM PGQ OMCDTPGB, PIK

NEITHER COLD NOR HOT I WILL SPUT THEE
IDAQRDG HNOK ING RNQ, A TAOO WEMD QRDD

OUT OF MY MOUTH
NMQ NX BJ BNMQR.

REVELATION
GDUDOPQANI 3:16   Clue: O = L

HE THAT OVERCOMETH THE SAME SHALL BE
AN ZAHZ MPNFGMKNZA, ZAN IHKN IAHOO DN

CLOTHED IN WHITE RAIMENT AND I WILL NOT
GOMZANR UE BAUZN FHUKNEZ; HER U BUOO EMZ

BLOT OUT HIS NAME OUT OF THE BOOK OF
DOMZ MCZ AUI EHKN MCZ MT ZAN DMMQ MT

LIFE BUT I WILL CONFESS HIS NAME BEFORE MY
OUTN, DCZ U BUOO GMETNII AUI EHKN DNTMFN KX

FATHER AND BEFORE HIS ANGELS
THZANF, HER DNTMFN AUI HEYNOI.

REVELATION
FNPNOHZUME 3:5   Clue: T = F

45 *Animals of the Bible*

(handwritten: EVERY THREE YEARS ONCE CAME THE SHIPS OF)
VWVTI RBTVV IVNTF CUGV GNPV RBV FBSMF CE

(handwritten: T SHASH BRINGING OLD AND SILVER IVORY AND)
(handwritten: TARSHISH)
RNTFBSFB HTSUJSUJ JCYL, NUL FSYWVT, SWCTI, NUL

(handwritten: APES AND PEACOCKS)
NMVF, NUL MVNGCGOF.

(handwritten: CHRONICLES)
2 GBTCUSGYVF 9:21

(handwritten: CORINTHIAN)

Clue: S = I

(handwritten: Chronicles)

(handwritten: THE WOLF ALSO SHALL DWELL WITH THE LAMB AND THE)
KYV PLEX FEUL UYFEE NPVEE PDKY KYV EFSW, FCN KYV

(handwritten: LEOPARD SHALL LIE DOWN WITH THE KID)
EVLJFON UYFEE EDV NLPC PDKY KYV HDN;

(handwritten: AND THE CALF AND THE YOUNG LION AND THE FATLING)
FCN KYV QFEX FCN KYV TLZCB EDLC FCN KYV XFKEDCB

(handwritten: TOGETHER AND A LITTLE CHILD SHALL LEAD THEM)
KLBVKYVO; FCN F EDKKEV QYDEN UYFEE EVFN KYVS.

DUFDFY 11:6
(handwritten: ISAIAH)

Clue: L = O

46 — Miracles of Paul

CGL DYL SKYVDWO AUTFECP NEKCFPTA HQ OWT

WCGLA YB UCVP: AY OWCO BKYN WEA HYLQ STKT

HKYVDWO VGOY OWT AEFI WCGLITKFWETBA YK CUKYGA,

CGL OWT LEATCATA LTUCKOTL BKYN OWTN, CGL OWT

TREP AUEKEOA STGO YVO YB OWTN.

CFOA 19:11–12 *(ACTS)* *Clue: V = U*

BAK DS NBEI SR YBHH, SMBS SMI TBSMIG RT YJOZDJH

ZBL HDNP RT B TIXIG BAK RT B OZRRKL TZJQ: SR FMRE

YBJZ IASIGIK DA, BAK YGBLIK, BAK ZBDK MDH MBAKH

RA MDE, BAK MIBZIK MDE.

BNSH 28:8 *(ACTS)* *Clue: Y = P*

Proverbially Speaking, Part 1

47

WHEN WISDOM ENTERETH INTO THINE HEART
MQVY MBHZRJ VYWVAVWQ BYWR WQBYV QVNAW,

AND KNOWLEDGE IS PLEASANT UNTO THY
NYZ CYRMOVZIV BH GOVNHNYW DYWR WQK

SOUL DISCRETION SHALL PRESERVE THEE
HRDO; ZBHFAVWBRY HQNOO GAVHVASV WQVV,

UNDERSTANDING SHALL KEEP THEE
DYZVAHWNYZBYI HQNOO CVVG WQVV.

GARSVAUH 2:10–11
PROVERBS

Clue: O = L

THE BLESSING OF THE LORD IT MAKETH RICH AND
CRU PWUKKBGZ NJ CRU WNLI, BC HTAUCR LBSR, TGI

HE ADDETH NO SORROW WITH IT
RU TIIUCR GN KNLLND DBCR BC.
Addeth

FLNEULPK 10:22
PROVERBS

Clue: N = O

Proverbially Speaking, Part 2

48

HOW MUCH BETTER IS IT TO GET WISDOM THAN
NVY UGHN MAOOAS DK DO OV XAO YDKWVU ONPJ

GOLD! AND TO GET UNDERSTANDING RATHER TO BE
XVBW! PJW OV XAO GJWASKOPJWDJX SPONAS OV MA

CHOSEN THAN SILVER!
HNVKAJ ONPJ KDBIAS!

ZSVIASMK 16:16   *Clue: K = S*
PROVERBS

MAKE NO FRIENDSHIP WITH AN ANGRY MAN AND WITH
UTEK PS DBOKPWLZOI XOCZ TP TPABM UTP; TPW XOCZ

A FURIOUS MAN THOU SHALT NOT GO LEST THOU
T DNBOSNL UTP CZSN LZTRC PSC AS: RKLC CZSN

LEARN HIS DAYS AND GET A SHARE TO THY SOUL
RKTBP ZOL XTML, TPW AKC T LPTBK CS CZM LSNR.

IBSGKBJL 22:24–25   *Clue: R = L*
PROVERBS

Ex-Queens

49

AND THE KING LOVED ESTHER ABOVE ALL THE
HOU LRM IAOD EVPMU MWLRMY HQVPM HEE LRM

WOMEN AND SHE OBTAINED GRACE AND FAVOUR
TVGMO, HOU WRM VQLHAOMU DYHJM HOU KHPVCY

IN HIS SIGHT MORE THAN ALL THE VIRGINS SO
AO RAW WADRL GVYM LRHO HEE LRM PAYDAOW; WV

THAT HE SET THE ROYAL CROWN UPON HER HEAD
LRHL RM WML LRM YVNHE JYVTO CZVO RMY RMHU,

AND MADE HER QUEEN INSTEAD OF VASHTI
HOU GHUM RMY FCMMO AOWLMHU VK PHWRLA.

MWLRMY 2:17
ESTHER

Clue: E = L

WHEREFORE THEY ⚓ AGAIN AND TOLD HI AND
YMAUAECUA KMAZ NSJA SPSFO, SOI KCDI MFJ. SOI

HE SAID THIS IS THE WORD OF THE LORDWHICH
MA BSFI, KMFB FB KMA YCUI CE KMA DCUI, YMFNM

HE SPAKE BE HIS SERVANT ELIJAH THE TISHBITE
MA BVSRA GZ MFB BAUXSOK ADFLSM KMA KFBMGFKA,

SAYING IN THE ORTION OFJE P LSHALL DOGS
BSZFOP, FO KMA VCUKFCO CE LAHUAAD BMSDD ICPB

EAT THE FLESH OF JEZEBEL
ASK KMA EDABM CE LAHAGAD.

2 RFOPB 9:36
KINGS

Clue: L = J

A Note from Jude

BELOVED, WHEN I GAVE ALL DILIGENCE TO WRITE UNTO
PBOLEBW, HIBY T JKEB KOO WTOTJBYDB SL HCTSB AYSL

YOU OF THE COMMON SALVATION IT WAS NEEDFUL
ULA LQ SIB DLVVLY MKOEKSTLY, TS HKM YBBWQAO

FOR ME TO WRITE UNTO YOU AND EXHORT YOU THAT YE
QLC VB SL HCTSB AYSL ULA, KYW BNILCS ULA SIKS UB

SHOULD EARNESTLY CONTEND FOR THE FAITH WHICH
MILAOW BKCYBMSOU DLYSBYW QLC SIB QKTSI HITDI

WAS ONCE DELIVERED UNTO THE SAINTS
HKM LYDB WBOTEBCBW AYSL SIB MKTYSM.

JUDE
XAWB 1:3   *Clue: A = U*

NOT UNTO HIM THAT IS ABLE TO KEEP YOU
JGF YJWG ZLT WZXW LA XNUO WG IOOS QGY

FROM FALLING AND TO PRESENT YOU FAULTLESS
PMGT PXUULJR, XJE WG SMOAOJW QGY PXYUWUOAA

BEFORE THE PRESENCE OF HIS GLORY WITH
NOPGMO WZO SMOAOJVO GP ZLA RUGMQ FLWZ

EXCEEDING JOY TO THE ONLY WISE GOD OUR
OBVOOELJR CGQ, WG WZO GJUQ FLAO RGE GYM

SAVIOUR BE GLORY AND MAJESTY DOMINION AND
AXDLGYM, NO RUGMQ XJE TXCOAWQ, EGTLJLGJ XJE

POWER
SGFOM.

CYEO 1:24–25   *Clue: N = B*
JUDE

51 Ezekiel's Visions

THE HAND OF THE LORD WAS UPON ME AND CARRIED
NKB KOUP EV NKB IEFP GOR CZEU AB, OUP MOFFYBP

ME OUT IN THE SPIRIT OF THE LORD, AND SET ME
AB ECN YU NKB RZYFYN EV NKB IEFP, OUP RBN AB

DOWN IN THE MIDST OF THE VALLEY WHICH WAS FULL
PEGU YU NKB AYPRN EV NKB LOIIBH GKYMK GOR VCII

OF BONES
EV XEUBR.

BQBJYBI 37:1
EZEKIEL

Clue: P = D

AND I LOOKE AND BEHOLD A HI   WIND CAME OUT O
IBS O WTTVMS, IBS, UMYTWS, I JYOKWJOBS ZILM TEC TH

THE   GRE CLOU AN A   E NFO NG
CYM BTKCY, I PKMIC ZWTES, IBS I HOKM OBHTWSOBP

ITSEL AND A BRIGHTNESS AS ABOUT IT AND OUT
OCNMWH, IBS I UKOPYCBMNN JIN IUTEC OC, IBS TEC

OF THE MIDS THEREO A THE COLOUR O A BER
TH CYM LOSNC CYMKMTH IN CYM ZTWTEK TH ILUMK,

OUT OF THE MIDST OF THE FIRE ALS OUT OF
TEC TH CYM LOSNC TH CYM HOKM. IWNT TEC TH

THE MI ST THERE F CAME THE   LIKENESS OF
CYM LOSNC CYMKMTH ZILM CYM WOVMBMNN TH

FOUR L IN CREATURES AN T IS A THEIR
HTEK WOROBP ZKMICEKMN. IBS CYON JIN CYMOK

A EARAN E THE   HD THE LIKENESS OF A MAN
IXXMIKIBZM; CYMG YIS CYM WOVMBMNN TH I LIB.

MAMVOMW 1:4–5
EZEKIEL

Clue: Z = C

On the Menu

DYF FUNY GUN XUMIFKNY PC MLKDNI LDE MG,

GUNW LDMF PYN GP DYPGUNK, MG ML TDYYD: CPK

GUNW EMLG YPG EUDG MG EDL. DYF TPLNL LDMF

VYGP GUNT, GUML ML GUN RKNDF EUMXU GUN IPKF

UDGU BMONY WPV GP NDG.

NHPFVL 16:15   *Clue: E = W*

———————————

HCG BDFC XHA IEDVFYG XKVF IHJYE'A FHKP, HCG XKVF

H WKPGEY DU H AOKC HTDNV FKA EDKCA; HCG FY

GKG YHV EDINAVA HCG XKEG FDCYR.

JHPO 1:6   *Clue: I = C*

Off the Menu

PT WVGZZ JCD TGD CE GJPDVAJI DVGD SATDV CE

ADWTZE: DVCL WVGZD IART AD LJDC DVT WDQGJITQ

DVGD AW AJ DVP IGDTW, DVGD VT BGP TGD AD.

STLDTQCJCBP 14:21   *Clue: J = N*

_____

RMO BEH DSTMH, BEFZJE EH OTGTOH BEH EFFK, RMO

QH NWFGHMKFFBHO, PHB EH NEHSHBE MFB BEH

NZO; EH TD ZMNWHRM BF PFZ.

WHGTBTNZD 11:7   *Clue: N = C*

54 Modes of Transportation

FWKK MW FYW EICSYFWL JA UTJR, XWYJKE, FYM HTRS

GJVWFY CRFJ FYWW, VWWH, IRE UTFFTRS COJR IR IUU,

IRE I GJKF FYW AJIK JA IR IUU.

VIFFYWN 21:5   *Clue: E = D*

———

BAF UDKTYM OBFT ITBFC MJK PMBIJDL, BAF VTAL XY LD

OTTL JKIBTH MJK EBLMTI, LD QDKMTA, BAF YITKTALTF

MJOKTHE XALD MJO; BAF MT ETHH DA MJK ATPZ, BAF

VTYL DA MJK ATPZ B QDDF VMJHT.

QTATKJK 46:29   *Clue: V = W*

55   *2 Corinthians*

IRAMG IG MYYZ CYS NS SRG SRACPQ IRAKR NWG

QGGC, UDS NS SRG SRACPQ IRAKR NWG CYS

QGGC: VYW SRG SRACPQ IRAKR NWG QGGC NWG

SGOEYWNM; UDS SRG SRACPQ IRAKR NWG CYS

QGGC NWG GSGWCNM.

2 KYWACSRANCQ 4:18   *Clue: Y = O*

———————

PVCYDTP SHGFBPJLPB, QOPMOPF SP UP DT MOP

KCDMO; IFHLP SHGF HQT BPJLPB. ETHQ SP THM SHGF

HQT BPJLPB, OHQ MOCM XPBGB NOFDBM DB DT SHG,

PVNPIM SP UP FPIFHUCMPB?

2 NHFDTMODCTB 13:5   *Clue: U = B*

56 The Number of Perfection

BOZ NEZ IHYAAYZ URY AYSYOUR ZBP, BOZ

ABOQUCMCYZ CU: IYQBLAY URBU CO CU RY RBZ

VYAUYZ MVEF BHH RCA XEVW XRCQR NEZ QVYBUYZ

BOZ FBZY.

NYOYACA 2:3   *Clue: R = H*

_____

JFY WPRHR BJVR DFWC VR CFR CI WPR ORXRF JFSRGO

QPMBP PJY WPR ORXRF XMJGO IDGG CI WPR ORXRF

GJOW EGJSDRO, JFY WJGARY QMWP VR, OJTMFS, BCVR

PMWPRH, M QMGG OPRQ WPRR WPR ZHMYR, WPR

GJVZ'O QMIR.

HRXRGJWMCF 21:9   *Clue: Z = B*

57 Poor Job, Part 1

CAE LOT PJWE GCFE MALJ GCLCA, OCGL LOJM

YJAGFETWTE ZK GTWBCAL NJH, LOCL LOTWT FG

AJAT PFIT OFZ FA LOT TCWLO, C DTWUTYL CAE

CA MDWFXOL ZCA, JAT LOCL UTCWTLO XJE, CAE

TGYOTQTLO TBFP?

NJH 1:8 *Clue: M = U*

_____

WKRT ACWCT CTADRBRM WKR XSBM, CTM ACJM,

MSWK ESO HRCB VSM HSB TSGVKW? KCAW TSW

WKSG UCMR CT KRMVR COSGW KJU, CTM COSGW

KJA KSGAR, CTM COSGW CXX WKCW KR KCWK ST

RYRBL AJMR?

ESO 1:9–10 *Clue: A = S*

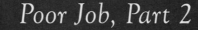

58 — *Poor Job, Part 2*

TE RUMO TWR CEBY BKRU UKS AQEY RUM

JFEAYC TMNMY CWOT WYC TMNMY YKJURT, WYC

YEYM TQWXM W BEFC AYRE UKS: VEF RUMO TWB

RUWR UKT JFKMV BWT NMFO JFMWR.

GEI 2:13   *Clue: J = G*

_____

GOMU YNC WPNHM, WUE PMUG ODH VWUGBM,

WUE HOWLME ODH OMWE, WUE KMBB ENSU IZNU

GOM XPNIUE, WUE SNPHODZZME, WUE HWDE, UWJME

RWVM D NIG NK VT VNGOMP'H SNVC, WUE UWJME

HOWBB D PMGIPU GODGOMP: GOM BNPE XWLM,

WUE GOM BNPE OWGO GWJMU WSWT.

YNC 1:20–21   *Clue: V = M*

59   *Job Restored*

AUKT SYW ETRVKIKO AUK XYIO, ETO REHO, H

DTYV AUEA AUYZ NETRA OY KGKIF AUHTJ, ETO AUEA

TY AUYZJUA NET WK VHAUUYXOKT LIYQ AUKK.

SYW 42:1–2   *Clue: H = I*

––––––––––

LR HUS KRME VKSLLSE HUS KFHHSM SYE RA GRV

ZRMS HUFY UBL VSJBYYBYJ: ARM US UFE ARQMHSSY

HURQLFYE LUSSD, FYE LBC HURQLFYE NFZSKL, FYE F

HURQLFYE WRTS RA RCSY, FYE F HURQLFYE LUS FLLSL.

US UFE FKLR LSXSY LRYL LRYL FYE HUMSS EFQJUHSML.

GRV 42:12–13   *Clue: V = B*

60 *The Crucifixion*

LAS ZPRA KPRU ZRCR DIWR KI KPR FTLDR, ZPGDP GY

DLTTRS DLTJLCU, KPRCR KPRU DCEDGBGRS PGW, LAS KPR

WLTRBLDKICY, IAR IA KPR CGNPK PLAS, LAS KPR IKPRC

IA KPR TRBK.

TEHR 23:33   *Clue:* Z = W

———————

HVU HQOFM OPHO OPFL PHU BSRCFU PYB, OPFL

OSSC OPF MSXF SQQ QMSB PYB, HVU GZO PYJ SEV

MHYBFVO SV PYB, HVU IFU PYB HEHL OS RMZRYQL

PYB. HVU HJ OPFL RHBF SZO, OPFL QSZVU H BHV SQ

RLMFVF, JYBSV XL VHBF: PYB OPFL RSBGFIIFU OS XFHM

PYJ RMSJJ.

BHOOPFE 27:31–32   *Clue:* R = C

Gideon

STBUPJ, F EFPP VXC H WPTTAT UW EUUP FR CBT WPUUI;

HRJ FW CBT JTE ST UR CBT WPTTAT URPN, HRJ FC ST

JIN XVUR HPP CBT THICB STYFJT, CBTR YBHPP F QRUE

CBHC CBUX EFPC YHGT FYIHTP SN DFRT BHRJ, HY CBUX

BHYC YHFJ.

OXJZTY 6:37   *Clue: S = B*

EKY CFI CFQII WTADEKSIJ LRIB CFI CQGADICJ, EKY

LQEXI CFI DSCWFIQJ, EKY FIRY CFI READJ SK CFISQ

RINC FEKYJ, EKY CFI CQGADICJ SK CFISQ QSZFC FEKYJ

CT LRTB BSCFER: EKY CFIV WQSIY, CFI JBTQY TN CFI

RTQY, EKY TN ZSYITK.

MGYZIJ 7:20   *Clue: B = W*

62 *Temptation*

FWIBI WYFW HN FIUZFYFLNH FYMIH SNV PVF EVOW

YE LE ONUUNH FN UYH: PVF ANR LE KYLFWKVX, CWN

CLXX HNF EVKKIB SNV FN PI FIUZFIR YPNDI FWYF SI

YBI YPXI; PVF CLXX CLFW FWI FIUZFYFLNH YXEN UYMI Y

CYS FN IEOYZI, FWYF SI UYS PI YPXI FN PIYB LF.

1 ONBLHFWIYHE 10:13   *Clue: K = F*

ZT REZTL, ZT CYWYJXGH; ZTAXQRT BEQL XFCTLRXLB HMT

FTCYJ, XR X LEXLYGW JYEG, KXJPTHM XZEQH, RTTPYGW

KMED MT DXB FTCEQL: KMED LTRYRH RHTFUXRH YG

HMT UXYHM.

1 VTHTL 5:8–9   *Clue: F = D*

63 · Framed!

JWL JPJN IJRF BWCA PBK PAEKF PFJUD JWL LBKVMFJKFL

NFIJEKF AZ CPF TAXL TPBIP WJNACP CPF GFYXFFMBCF PJL

KVAQFW CA PBR: ZAX PF PJL KJBL, B TBMM WAC HBUF

CPFF CPF BWPFXBCJWIF AZ RD ZJCPFXK.... NEC GFYFNFM

PBK TBZF IJRF CA PBR, JWL KJBL EWCA PBR, TPD BK CPD

KVBXBC KA KJL, CPJC CPAE FJCFKC WA NXFJL?

1 QBWHK 21:4–5   *Clue: I = C*

_____

XCEAOUPZ U GUVW, UJI VLW JUSEWY EJ YPDY UZEJD

WYL XLEXOL: UJI VLW WKE ZLJ, VEJV EG SLOPUO,

SLGECL YPZ, WE SLUC KPWJLVV UDUPJVW YPZ, VUHPJD,

WYEB IPIVW SOUVXYLZL DEI UJI WYL RPJD. UJI WYLJ

AUCCH YPZ EBW, UJI VWEJL YPZ.

1 RPJDV 21:9–10   *Clue: O = L*

KJFBW LHORJN GCO GE OYFBR GLB QFNORJB, HBK

JCBBFBP LHORJN GCO GE OYFBR GLB LRDD.

UJGTRJIN 5:15   *Clue: F = I*

_____

FAO ONQ GECXOJWX VA VFADDAL: JXL TABEWUA

KWON ONA KWGA EG ONQ QECON. FAO NAT VA

JD ONA FEZWXS NWXL JXL IFAJDJXO TEA; FAO NAT

VTAJDOD DJOWDGQ ONAA JO JFF OWHAD; JXL VA

ONEC TJZWDNAL JFKJQD KWON NAT FEZA.

ITEZATVD 5:18–19   *Clue: L = D*

65 — From the Book of Galatians

TWGEZP WHPW GSKSSYSK AZ CGDY PWS TAGZS DC

PWS JHO, VSEBX YHKS H TAGZS CDG AZ: CDG EP EZ

OGEPPSB, TAGZSK EZ SRSGN DBS PWHP WHBXSPW DB

H PGSS.

XHJHPEHBZ 3:13   *Clue: E = I*

FAYTEAB NCMN M KMA EV AYN WPVNEIEGJ LQ NCG

TYHFV YI NCG UMT, LPN LQ NCG IMENC YI WGVPV

ZCHEVN, GOGA TG CMOG LGUEGOGJ EA WGVPV

ZCHEVN, NCMN TG KEBCN LG WPVNEIEGJ LQ NCG

IMENC YI ZCHEVN, MAJ AYN LQ NCG TYHFV YI NCG

UMT: IYH LQ NCG TYHFV YI NCG UMT VCMUU AY

IUGVC LG WPVNEIEGJ.

BMUMNEMAV 2:16   *Clue: F = K*

66 Snakes in the Bible

BMOWOCFWO BMO ROFRHO UYSO BF SFAOA, YIP

AYXP, GO MYNO AXIIOP, CFW GO MYNO ARFJOI

YEYXIAB BMO HFWP, YIP YEYXIAB BMOO; RWYQ VIBF

BMO HFWP, BMYB MO BYJO YGYQ BMO AOWROIBA

CWFS VA. YIP SFAOA RWYQOP CFW BMO ROFRHO.

IVSZOWA 21:7   *Clue: R = P*

———————

UIC FBKI LUOT BUC DUABKYKC U POICTK QN ZAGHEZ,

UIC TUGC ABKS QI ABK NGYK, ABKYK HUSK U JGLKY

QOA QN ABK BKUA, UIC NUZAKIKC QI BGZ BUIC.

UHAZ 28:3   *Clue: T = L*

67 True Beauty

UPL OTG VAGB T QASNELEI ULYTG? VLS PFS MSAOF AI

VTS TDLQF SEDAFI. NPF PFTSN LV PFS PEIDTGB BLNP

ITVFCZ NSEIN AG PFS, IL NPTN PF IPTCC PTQF GL GFFB

LV IMLAC.

MSLQFSDI 31:10–11

Clue: E = U

NDWXB YLWICHCM RBU HU CWU TB UDYU WSUNYIL

YLWICHCM WJ QRYHUHCM UDB DYHI, YCL WJ

NBYIHCM WJ MWRL, WI WJ QSUUHCM WC WJ

YQQYIBR; TSU RBU HU TB UDB DHLLBC AYC WJ UDB

DBYIU, HC UDYU NDHKD HX CWU KWIISQUHTRB, BGBC

UDB WICYABCU WJ Y ABBP YCL OSHBU XQHIHU.

1 QBUBI 3:3–4

Clue: Q = P

68   *A Little R & R*

IAL XCLLM FQ O COVFWKZUE POU ZX XDLLI, DALIALK

AL LOI CZIICL FK PWNA: VWI IAL OVWUHOUNL FQ IAL

KZNA DZCC UFI XWQQLK AZP IF XCLLM.

LNNCLXZOXILX 5:12   *Clue: X = S*

———————

UEY GK NUMY HEBL BGKQ, ILQK SK SLHONKCXKN

UDUOB MEBL U YKNKOB DCUIK, UEY OKNB U FGMCK:

ZLO BGKOK FKOK QUES ILQMEA UEY ALMEA, UEY

BGKS GUY EL CKMNHOK NL QHIG UN BL KUB.

QUOV 6:31   *Clue: Q = M*

69 Quotable Exodus

C TY VLS GRFH VLA DRH, JLCPL LTES IFRNDLV VLSS RNV

RM VLS GTZH RM SDAXV, RNV RM VLS LRNWS RM

IRZHTDS. VLRN WLTGV LTES ZR RVLSF DRHW ISMRFS YS.

SQRHNW 20:2–3   *Clue: D = G*

———————————

NVU TY ANRU, R CRII ONFY NII OJ XLLUVYAA SNAA

PYQLKY ETYY, NVU R CRII SKLBINRO ETY VNOY LQ ETY

ILKU PYQLKY ETYY; NVU CRII PY XKNBRLWA EL CTLO R

CRII PY XKNBRLWA, NVU CRII ATYC OYKBJ LV CTLO R

CRII ATYC OYKBJ.

YZLUWA 33:19   *Clue: P = B*

Friends of Jesus

CFV DOLXL KFJON ZEPASE, ECN SOP LTLAOP, ECN

KEREPXL. VSOC SO SEN SOEPN ASOPOIFPO ASEA SO

VEL LTBH, SO EWFNO AVF NEQL LATKK TC ASO LEZO

YKEBO VSOPO SO VEL.

DFSC 11:5–6   *Clue: L = S*

_____

HSV HD WAV WFH FALGA AVJUO QHAS NBVJY,

JSO DHCCHFVO ALT, FJN JSOUVF, NLTHS BVWVU'N

PUHWAVU. AV DLUNW DLSOVWA ALN HFS PUHWAVU

NLTHS, JSO NJLWA KSWH ALT, FV AJXV DHKSO WAV

TVNNLJN, FALGA LN, PVLSE LSWVUBUVWVO, WAV

GAULNW.

QHAS 1:40–41   *Clue: G = C*

71 Animal Miracles

BQP DES WMGP MCSQSP DES NMRDE MT DES BII, BQP

IES IBJP RQDM OBWBBN, LEBD EBZS J PMQS RQDM

DESS, DEBD DEMR EBID INJDDSQ NS DESIS DEGSS

DJNSI?

QRNOSGI 22:28

Clue: J = I

OHERCEYAEIOMCOU, WDAE RD AYHJWM HBBDOM

EYDS, UH EYHJ EH EYD ADI, IOM QIAE IO YHHV,

IOM EIVD JZ EYD BCAY EYIE BCXAE QHSDEY JZ; IOM

RYDO EYHJ YIAE HZDODM YCA SHJEY, EYHJ AYIWE

BCOM I ZCDQD HB SHODK: EYIE EIVD, IOM UCND

JOEH EYDS BHX SD IOM EYDD.

SIEEYDR 17:27

Clue: U = G

Secretaries

WSMX KMTMJNDS RDUUMI LDTBRS WSM GAX AY

XMTNDS: DXI LDTBRS ETAWM YTAJ WSM JABWS AY

KMTMJNDS DUU WSM EATIG AY WSM UATI, ESNRS SM

SDI GCAQMX BXWA SNJ, BCAX D TAUU AY D LAAQ.

KMTMJNDS 36:4   *Clue: J = M*

D BCGBDSR, AMI AGIBC BMDR CTDRBOC, RWOSBC XIS

DF BMC OIGQ.

GIKWFR 16:22   *Clue: O = L*

73 The Night Sky

KSOPS DNQRJS NVPJBVBC, GVOGL, NLA YTRONARC,

NLA JSR PSNDFRVC GE JSR CGBJS. KSOPS AGRJS XVRNJ

JSOLXC YNCJ EOLAOLX GBJ; MRN, NLA KGLARVC

KOJSGBJ LBDFRV.

ZGF 9:9–10

Clue: O = I

CSMTMOYTM GKTFLI CSMTM MBML YO YLM, FLR SDA FG

IYYR FG RMFR, GY AFLZ FG CSM GCFTG YO CSM GVZ DL

ANXCDCNRM, FLR FG CSM GFLR ESDHS DG PZ CSM GMF

GSYTM DLLNAMTFPXM.

SMPTMEG 11:12

Clue: R = D

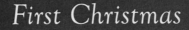

First Christmas

WAG JZZ LRNH GJH BAWP, LRJL NL FNVRL OP

MXZMNZZPB GRNQR GJH HIAYPW AM LRP ZAKB OT LRP

IKAIRPL, HJTNWV, OPRAZB, J CNKVNW HRJZZ OP GNLR

QRNZB, JWB HRJZZ OKNWV MAKLR J HAW, JWB LRPT

HRJZZ QJZZ RNH WJFP PFFJWXPZ.

FJLLRPG 1:22–23   *Clue: V = G*

SXQ IH UE CSI, ETSE, CTUZF ETFJ CFGF ETFGF, ETF QSJI

CFGF SKKHALZUITFQ ETSE ITF ITHRZQ OF QFZUNFGFQ.

SXQ ITF OGHRMTE VHGET TFG VUGIEOHGX IHX, SXQ

CGSLLFQ TUA UX ICSQQZUXM KZHETFI, SXQ ZSUQ TUA

UX S ASXMFG; OFKSRIF ETFGF CSI XH GHHA VHG ETFA

UX ETF UXX.

ZRWF 2:6–7   *Clue: Z = L*

Shadrach, Meshach, and Abednego

KM KR PT IN, NOW ANF UCNL UT ITWQT KI ZPST RN

FTSKQTW OI MWNL RCT POWEKEA MKTWB MOWEZHT,

ZEF CT UKSS FTSKQTW OI NOR NM RCKET CZEF, N

GKEA. POR KM ENR, PT KR GENUE OERN RCTT, N GKEA,

RCZR UT UKSS ENR ITWQT RCB ANFI, ENW UNWICKX

RCT ANSFTE KLZAT UCKHC RCNO CZIR ITR OX.

FZEKTS 3:17–18

Clue: U = W

HGT WSJ OQUGMJI, NEZJQGEQI, HGT MHOWHUGI,

HGT WSJ LUGN'I MEPGIJRREQI, AJUGN NHWSJQJT

WENJWSJQ, IHK WSJIJ VJG, POEG KSEIJ AETUJI WSJ

BUQJ SHT GE OEKJQ, GEQ KHI HG SHUQ EB WSJUQ

SJHT IUGNJT, GJUWSJQ KJQJ WSJUQ MEHWI MSHGNJT,

GEQ WSJ IVJRR EB BUQJ SHT OHIIJT EG WSJV.

THGUJR 3:27

Clue: M = C

RJAKGB MKD RJAJWKIA, DALVA L WFBJ DLIA IAJJ; AJ

JFIJIA TCFUU FU FM KS.

NKR 40:15   *Clue: K = O*

DW MXTM FTZ MXL SCUF PDMX XDO OCUL TWF HULTM

TWF OMUCWH OPCUF OXTSS JYWDOX SLQDTMXTW

MXL JDLUKDWH OLUJLWM, LQLW SLQDTMXTW MXTM

KUCCRLF OLUJLWM; TWF XL OXTSS OSTZ MXL FUTHCW

MXTM DO DW MXL OLT.

DOTDTX 27:1   *Clue: J = P*

77 — The Fall of Jericho

HMO LJAE YLLADXE OANLDTEAO HXX LJHL GHN RM LJA

PRLE, VTLJ ZHM HMO GTZHM, ETYMI HMO TXO, HMO

TK, HMO NJAAC, HMO HNN, GRLJ LJA AOIA TU LJA

NGTDO.

STNJYH 6:21

Clue: L = T

GKS CF HWGUU ABQL FB XGHH, FWGF PWLK FWLM

QGIL G UBKY TUGHF PCFW FWL EGQ'H WBEK, GKS

PWLK ML WLGE FWL HBNKS BZ FWL FENQXLF, GUU

FWL XLBXUL HWGUU HWBNF PCFW G YELGF HWBNF;

GKS FWL PGUU BZ FWL ACFM HWGUU ZGUU SBPK

ZUGF, GKS FWL XLBXUL HWGUU GHALKS NX LJLEM

QGK HFEGCYWF TLZBEL WCQ.

RBHWNG 6:5

Clue: Q = M

78   *Hosea*

VSJY DWOU VSJ KAMU PYVA TJ, HA IJV, KAGJ

W RATWY NJKAGJU AC SJM CMOJYU, IJV WY

WUPKVJMJDD, WLLAMUOYH VA VSJ KAGJ AC VSJ KAMU

VARWMU VSJ LSOKUMJY AC ODMWJK, RSA KAAX VA

AVSJM HAUD, WYU KAGJ CKWHAYD AC ROYJ.

SADJW 3:1.

Clue: S = H

C OCWW KJMW VKJCA XMENBWCRCGI, C OCWW

WDPJ VKJS HAJJWZ: HDA SCGJ MGIJA CB VLAGJR

MOMZ HADS KCS. C OCWW XJ MB VKJ RJO LGVD

CBAMJW: KJ BKMWW IADO MB VKJ WCWZ, MGR

EMBV HDAVK KCB ADDVB MB WJXMGDG.

KDBJM 14:4–5

Clue: D = O

79 Money, Money, Money

LPW LEJLMLN MSLJZSPSW OPBI SVMJIP; LPW LEJLMLN

YSTQMSW BI SVMJIP BMS FTUXSJ, YMTHM MS MLW

PLNSW TP BMS LOWTSPHS IR BMS FIPF IR MSBM, RIOJ

MOPWJSW FMSZSUF IR FTUXSJ, HOJJSPB NIPSC YTBM

BMS NSJHMLPB.

QSPSFTF 23:16   *Clue: T = I*

_____

FRL CDABA AFH QWDE FVFGRAH HSD HEDFABEZ, FRL

XDSDNL SQM HSD UDQUND KFAH YQRDZ GRHQ HSD

HEDFABEZ: FRL YFRZ HSFH MDED EGKS KFAH GR YBKS.

FRL HSDED KFYD F KDEHFGR UQQE MGLQM, FRL ASD

HSEDM GR HMQ YGHDA, MSGKS YFID F JFEHSGRV.

YFEI 12:41–42   *Clue: K = C*

80   *Get Saved!*

KRF GBWA WAS ASNFW VNL JSMBSESWA CLWR

FBZAWSRCTLSTT; NLH GBWA WAS VRCWA PRLKSTTBRL BT

VNHS CLWR TNMENWBRL.

FRVNLT 10:10   *Clue: F = R*

EMJWJODWJ, IA FJPDSJC, KV AJ MKSJ KPEKAV DFJAJC,

YDR KV GY IA XWJVJYBJ DYPA, FTR YDE ITBM IDWJ GY

IA KFVJYBJ, EDWQ DTR ADTW DEY VKPSKRGDY EGRM

OJKW KYC RWJIFPGYZ.

XMGPGXXGKYV 2:12   *Clue: F = B*

81) *Letter to Thessalonica*

ANQ INL SWTUYFV OAL NZH VOPSYH, OAL NZH FNHL

MYUZU GSHWUP, LWHYGP NZH QOJ ZAPN JNZ. OAL

PSY FNHL TOEY JNZ PN WAGHYOUY OAL OCNZAL WA

FNRY NAY PNQOHL OANPSYH, OAL PNQOHL OFF TYA,

YRYA OU QY LN PNQOHL JNZ.

1 PSYUUOFNAWOAU 3:11–12   *Clue: S = H*

———————————

HAE EL LUSAWG OAP, XWLGSWLH, EFWH GSLD GSFG

FWL PHWPVO, BADRAWG GSL RLLXVLDTHKLK, JPYYAWG

GSL ELFQ, XL YFGTLHG GAEFWK FVV DLH. JLL GSFG HAHL

WLHKLW LMTV RAW LMTV PHGA FHO DFH; XPG LMLW

RAVVAE GSFG ESTBS TJ NAAK, XAGS FDAHN OAPWJLVMLJ,

FHK GA FVV DLH.

1 GSLJJFVAHTFHJ 5:14–15   *Clue: Y = P*

82 *Familiar Phrases*

DLLI AL FW NJL FIIZL XM NJL LGL, JPBL AL KHBLQ NJL

WJFBXT XM NJG TPHEW.

IWFZA 17:8   *Clue: F = A*

WLZ BHWULSRK DLHNN NOEW YQ WLR ATOUR; BOWL

WLR ATOUR WTFRWLRP DLHNN WLRZ DOKF: ETP WLRZ

DLHNN DRR RZR WT RZR, BLRK WLR NTPC DLHNN

IPOKF HFHOK MOTK.

ODHOHL 52:8   *Clue: T = O*

83 *More Familiar Phrases*

CLR YN LB ALHA CYEE SEBHF CYAL OB? DRM QRC, YD

Y LREF OP ARQJVB, Y NLHEE JYZB VS ALB JLRNA.

XRU 13:19   *Clue: C = W*

———————————

GH GOW IWTL FWBTCW U TD IWTL, GOTG U CUXOG

XTUA GOW IWTL: U TC CTEW TSS GOUAXD GH TSS

CWA, GOTG U CUXOG FP TSS CWTAD DTJW DHCW.

1 BHVUAGOUTAD 9:22   *Clue: S = L*

84   *You Swine!*

BGK LI RBYK QGPD PLIH, VD. BGK NLIG PLIC NIFI XDHI

DQP, PLIC NIGP YGPD PLI LIFK DE RNYGI: BGK, AILDMK,

PLI NLDMI LIFK DE RNYGI FBG WYDMIGPMC KDNG B

RPIIZ ZMBXI YGPD PLI RIB, BGK ZIFYRLIK YG PLI NBPIFR.

HBPPLIN 8:32   *Clue: F = R*

———

HV H FKYKB PT LPBC UO H VYUOK'V VOPDG, VP UV H

THUE YPWHO YAUIA UV YUGAPDG CUVIEKGUPO.

MEPZKERV 11:22   *Clue: Y = W*

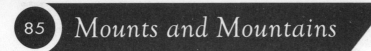

85 Mounts and Mountains

JSZ EIK JUW UKGEKZ TS EIK GKRKSEI VYSEI, YS EIK

GKRKSEKKSEI ZJH YA EIK VYSEI, PNYS EIK VYPSEJTSG YA

JUJUJE. JSZ EIK CJEKUG ZKOUKJGKZ OYSETSPJQQH PSETQ

EIK EKSEI VYSEI: TS EIK EKSEI VYSEI, YS EIK ATUGE ZJH

YA EIK VYSEI, CKUK EIK EYNG YA EIK VYPSEJTSG GKKS.

XKSKGTG 8:4–5   *Clue: J =A*

QFRSNO RU AN FYY DGOFNY XPRU AUXPR WFOANY,

FPB RSN EOUESNRG UV TFFY VUXO SXPBONB FPB

VDVRM, FPB RSN EOUESNRG UV RSN QOUZNG VUXO

SXPBONB, HSDWS NFR FR INJNTNY'G RFTYN. GU FSFT

GNPR XPRU FYY RSN WSDYBONP UV DGOFNY, FPB

QFRSNONB RSN EOUESNRG.

1 LDPQG 18:19–20   *Clue: Q = G*

86   *Bible Occupations*

HPCW AMPQPKRQP AR XRZZU, UCW GUJJ MSAMPQ

HSIRC, NMRHP HLQCUIP SH ZPAPQ; MP SH JRWDPW

SC AMP MRLHP RK RCP HSIRC U AUCCPQ EB AMP HPU

HSWP: NMR, NMPC MP GRIPAM, HMUJJ HZPUV LCAR

AMPP.

UGAH 10:32   *Clue: M = H*

YBMF KMTLT BMRCJ OH, BM TROHB LFHD HBMV,

HBMI HBRH RCM YBDEM BRXM FD FMMJ DG HBM

UBITOSORF, QLH HBMI HBRH RCM TOSW: O SRVM

FDH HD SREE HBM COZBHMDLT, QLH TOFFMCT HD

CMUMFHRFSM.

VRCW 2:17   *Clue: C = R*

87 · More Bible Occupations

RSUY PYGBUJUL PODG, PYL GPWL RD POPKWPS, W BPG

YD TJDTSUR, YUWRSUJ BPG W P TJDTSUR'G GDY; CVR

W BPG PY SUJLOPY, PYL P XPRSUJUJ DN GZHDODJU

NJVWR.

PODG 7:14   *Clue: S = H*

YWOWGDFXQ, H QFNKWDQOFGA, BAFMA OHYW

QFNKWD QADFZWQ LVD YFHZH, PDVXJAG ZV

QOHNN JHFZ XZGV GAW MDHLGQOWZ; BAVO AW

MHNNWY GVJWGAWD BFGA GAW BVDTOWZ VL NFTW

VMMXCHGFVZ, HZY QHFY, QFDQ, EW TZVB GAHG PE

GAFQ MDHLG BW AHKW VXD BWHNGA.

HMGQ 19:24–25   *Clue: M = C*

Even More
Bible Occupations

VD MD XNKXPDZ, A MD KENVXSZPDS; KAJU, A MD

LCSDZTDNNDTN, HAT RKD JKDXR XSZ HAT RKD VXTUDM;

VDOXEND RKD KXTLDNR AH RKD HCDUZ CN FDTCNKDZ.

WADU 1:11   *Clue: V = B*

————————

PUL ORQMQ QPGL MUJF JCR XRUJMTGFU, HF JCK

SPK; PUL PQ JCFM CPQJ NRZGRDRL, QF NR GJ LFUR

MUJF JCRR. PUL CGQ QRTDPUJ SPQ CRPZRL GU JCR

QRZYQPER CFMT.

EPJJCRS 8:13   *Clue: L = D*

89 *Theological Terms*

HXMAMOQAM JC PI HXM QOOMGWM QO

QGM URNLVMGH WJVM RBQG JEE VMG

HQ WQGNMVGJHSQG; MTMG CQ PI HXM

ASLXHMQRCGMCC QO QGM HXM OAMM LSOH WJVM

RBQG JEE VMG RGHQ URCHSOSWJHSQG QO ESOM.

AQVJGC 5:18   *Clue: J = A*

OAORG MRRDEZLSU GD GJO KDEOCSDBAOZUO DK

UDZ GJO KMGJOE, GJEDWUJ PMSRGLKLRMGLDS DK

GJO PVLELG, WSGD DFOZLOSRO MSZ PVELSCALSU DK

GJO FADDZ DK NOPWP RJELPG: UEMRO WSGD XDW,

MSZ VOMRO, FO HWAGLVALOZ.

1 VOGOE 1:2   *Clue: R = C*

90 · *Strong Women*

HKLD MCLN KLGLA'I YTQL HFFO C DCTN FQ HKL

HLDH, CDU HFFO CD KCZZLA TD KLA KCDU, CDU YLDH

IFQHNS PDHF KTZ, CDU IZFHL HKL DCTN TDHF KTI

HLZXNLI, CDU QCIHLDLU TH TDHF HKL WAFPDU: QFA KL

YCI QCIH CINLLX CDU YLCAS. IF KL UTLU.

MPUWLI 4:21   *Clue: I = S*

———————

SOM MIQGNSW, S BNGBWIUILL, UWI XPYI GY

CSBPMGUW, LWI EAMZIM PLNSIC SU UWSU UPHI. SOM

LWI MXICU AOMIN UWI BSCH UNII GY MIQGNSW

QIUXIIO NSHSW SOM QIUWIC PO HGAOU IBWNSPH:

SOM UWI RWPCMNIO GY PLNSIC RSHI AB UG WIN

YGN EAMZHIOU.

EAMZIL 4:4–5   *Clue: C = L*

91 Nehemiah's Story, Part 1

IGE F AIFE CGMK MRW QFGN, FB FM SXWIAW MRW

QFGN, IGE FB MRH AWLDIGM RIDW BKCGE BIDKCL

FG MRH AFNRM, MRIM MRKC YKCXEWAM AWGE PW

CGMK ZCEIR, CGMK MRW JFMH KB PH BIMRWLA'

AWSCXJRLWA, MRIM F PIH OCFXE FM.

GWRWPFIR 2:5   *Clue: E = D*

———————————

X MXFI, A PCVCCKL ULCC, MCU HXE ULAHC CRF PC

RUUCHUAGC UX ULC ZFRNCF XB ULN VCFGRHU, RHI UX

ULC ZFRNCF XB ULN VCFGRHUV, ELX ICVAFC UX BCRF ULN

HROC: RHI ZFXVZCF, A ZFRN ULCC, ULN VCFGRHU ULAV

IRN, RHI TFRHU LAO OCFKN AH ULC VATLU XB ULAV

ORH. BXF A ERV ULC DAHT'V KQZPCRFCF.

HCLCOARL 1:11   *Clue: Z = P*

Nehemiah's Story, Part 2

IRLD VRKJR FNKMALA TG IRL VUMM, UGA IRLD IRUI

FUBL FNBALGY, VKIR IRTYL IRUI MUALA, LSLBD TGL VKIR

TGL TW RKY RUGAY VBTNQRI KG IRL VTBX, UGA VKIR

IRL TIRLB RUGA RLMA U VLUZTG.

GLRLCKUR 4:17–18   *Clue: F = B*

———

KD LPJ OBFF OBK ERCRKPJG. . . . BCG RL MBQJ LD IBKK,

LPBL OPJC BFF DXW JCJQRJK PJBWG LPJWJDE, BCG BFF

LPJ PJBLPJC LPBL OJWJ BYDXL XK KBO LPJKJ LPRCUK, LPJN

OJWJ QXMP MBKL GDOC RC LPJRW DOC JNJK: EDW

LPJN IJWMJRHJG LPBL LPRK ODWZ OBK OWDXUPL DE

DXW UDG.

CJPJQRBP 6:15–16   *Clue: O = W*

Repent!

DWCQ PYTP PGQK VKMOM FKRTH PC ZWKTNY, THU PC

MTB, WKZKHP: DCW PYK XGHRUCQ CD YKTIKH GM TP

YTHU.

QTPPYKL 4:17   *Clue: Q = M*

———————

PU Y OYHS, UPYRC RCS OBXM TBM, Y CPHS JB

QOSPUFXS YJ RCS MSPRC BD RCS AYILSM; KFR RCPR

RCS AYILSM RFXJ DXBZ CYU APV PJM OYHS.

SGSLYSO 33:11   *Clue: H = V*

94   *Named Angels*

EJF BNPDP OET OED SJ NPEXPJ: ASZNEPY EJF NST

EJKPYT LUHKNB EKESJTB BNP FDEKUJ; EJF BNP FDEKUJ

LUHKNB EJF NST EJKPYT.

DPXPYEBSUJ 12:7   *Clue: F = D*

––––––––––

YSM VTF YSAFU YSIZFGJSA IYJM PSVL TJD, J YD

AYKGJFU, VTYV IVYSM JS VTF OGFIFSEF LC ALM; YSM

YD IFSV VL IOFYB PSVL VTFF, YSM VL ITFZ VTFF VTFIF

AUYM VJMJSAI.

UPBF 1:19   *Clue: J = I*

95   *Big Cats*

NOW HG FU SNH NU UVB DBZFOOFOZ GA UVBFP

WSBCCFOZ UVBPB, UVNU UVBQ ABNPBW OGU UVB

CGPW: UVBPBAGPB UVB CGPW HBOU CFGOH NIGOZ

UVBI, SVFEV HCBS HGIB GA UVBI.

2 XFOZH 17:25   *Clue:* Z = G

WYZ QMSY RMS OGTOMSR RMWR FGTHUMR MAI

FWDC KGTI RMS QWX MSWGZ RMSGSTK, MS LWAZ, AR

AL RMS IWY TK UTZ, QMT QWL ZALTFSZASYR HYRT RMS

QTGZ TK RMS NTGZ: RMSGSKTGS RMS NTGZ MWRM

ZSNAPSGSZ MAI HYRT RMS NATY, QMADM MWRM

RTGY MAI, WYZ LNWAY MAI.

1 CAYUL 13:26   *Clue:* N = L

96 — *Scripture on Scripture*

TJG VSP CJGK JT WJK BH UIBOX, YLK MJCPGTIR, YLK

HSYGMPG VSYL YLE VCJPKWPK HCJGK, MBPGOBLW PFPL

VJ VSP KBFBKBLW YHILKPG JT HJIR YLK HMBGBV, YLK

JT VSP ZJBLVH YLK AYGGJC, YLK BH Y KBHOPGLPG JT

VSP VSJIWSVH YLK BLVPLVH JT VSP SPYGV.

SPQGPCH 4:12   *Clue: C = W*

————————————

TSALGS! DFGB YGXBD, DFPD SA KXAKFQNC AY DFQ

BNXGKDHXQ GB AY PSC KXGJPDQ GSDQXKXQDPDGAS.

YAX DFQ KXAKFQNC NPZQ SAD GS AWM DGZQ RC

DFQ LGWW AY ZPS: RHD FAWC ZQS AY IAM BKPTQ PB

DFQC LQXQ ZAJQM RC DFQ FAWC IFABD.

2 KQDQX 1:20–21   *Clue: K = P*

Off to School

KQWLWTILW YQW APK KPE IHL EZQIIADPEYWL YI CLVFN

HE HFYI ZQLVEY, YQPY KW DVNQY CW UHEYVTVWB

CS TPVYQ. CHY PTYWL YQPY TPVYQ VE ZIDW, KW PLW

FI AIFNWL HFBWL P EZQIIADPEYWL.

NPAPYVPFE 3:24–25   *Clue: H = U*

———————

CNR XIYJ TZOYFP XYFY IGFTYJYT, GJT CYMZYOYT

JLR, CNR PQGSY YOZM LD RIGR XGU CYDLFY

RIY WNMRZRNTY, IY TYQGFRYT DFLW RIYW, GJT

PYQGFGRYT RIY TZPEZQMYP, TZPQNRZJB TGZMU ZJ RIY

PEILLM LD LJY RUFGJJNP.

GERP 19:9   *Clue: M = L*

98 *Elect Me!*

GPI UWC NWRFSICT QCRTM TPU KCU QPIT, TCRUWCI

WXZRTM SPTC XTK MPPS PI CZRF, UWXU UWC YJIYPLC

PG MPS XNNPISRTM UP CFCNURPT HRMWU LUXTS, TPU

PG VPIAL, QJU PG WRH UWXU NXFFCUW.

IPHXTL 9:11   *Clue: Q = B*

———————

FRTCTMDCT BRT CXBRTC, ACTBRCTS, VWUT NWZWVTSIT

BD QXET ODLC IXZZWSV XSN TZTIBWDS GLCT: MDC

WM OT ND BRTGT BRWSVG, OT GRXZZ STUTC MXZZ:

MDC GD XS TSBCXSIT GRXZZ AT QWSWGBTCTN LSBD

ODL XALSNXSBZO WSBD BRT TUTCZXGBWSV EWSVNDQ

DM DLC ZDCN XSN GXUWDLC YTGLG IRCWGB.

2 JTBTC 1:10–11   *Clue: U = V*

99 Tools in the Bible

GLT XL GSS FJSSP WFGW PFGSS ZU TJDDUT BJWF WFU

QGWWXOY, WFUVU PFGSS LXW OXQU WFJWFUV WFU

IUGV XI ZVJUVP GLT WFXVLP: ZCW JW PFGSS ZU IXV

WFU PULTJLD IXVWF XI XMUL, GLT IXV WFU WVUGTJLD

XI SUPPUV OGWWSU.

JPGJGF 7:25   *Clue: D = G*

———————

UQR PLY LKNJY, SLYQ MP SUJ MQ TNMBRMQH, SUJ

TNMBP KZ JPKQY CURY AYURE TYZKAY MP SUJ TAKNHLP

PLMPLYA: JK PLUP PLYAY SUJ QYMPLYA LUCCYA QKA UFY

QKA UQE PKKB KZ MAKQ LYUAR MP PLY LKNJY, SLMBY

MP SUJ MQ TNMBRMQH.

1 OMQHJ 6:7   *Clue: N = U*

100   *The Life of Peter*

MTQ JOBT DBSBY JMU VGIB QGJT GLS GP SOB UORD,

OB JMEFBQ GT SOB JMSBY, SG HG SG ZBULU.

IMSSOBJ 14:29   *Clue: M = A*

GBDK MDGDF OREP, OECWDF RKP NHCP BRWD E

KHKD; AQG OQJB RO E BRWD NEWD E GBDD: EK

GBD KRUD HL YDOQO JBFEOG HL KRTRFDGB FEOD QM

RKP SRCX.

RJGO 3:6   *Clue: H = O*

God's People

WS ZK XBDXOB, GPWHP FCB HFOOBN MK ZK AFZB,

LPFOO PRZMOB JPBZLBOYBL, FAN XCFK, FAN LBBT ZK

SFHB, FAN JRCA SCDZ JPBWC GWHTBN GFKL; JPBA

GWOO W PBFC SCDZ PBFYBA, FAN GWOO SDCQWYB

JPBWC LWA, FAN GWOO PBFO JPBWC OFAN.

2 HPCDAWHOBL 7:14   *Clue: C = R*

KWH FL JDL J ROENLG TLGLDJHVEG, J DEFJY

ADVLNHOEEU, JG OEYF GJHVEG, J ALRWYVJD ALEAYL.

1 ALHLD 2:9   *Clue: G = N*

Sacrifices

PYI PRGPKPL NQQU NKB VQQI QH NKB RWGYN

QHHBGOYA, PYI ZPOI ON WFQY OEPPD KOE EQY; PYI

KB NQQU NKB HOGB OY KOE KPYI, PYI P UYOHB; PYI

NKBS VBYN RQNK QH NKBL NQABNKBG.

ABYBEOE 22:6

Clue: R = B

JL RUD AUVPU AVNN AD KWD OKYPRVHVDS RUWXMIU

RUD XHHDWVYI XH RUD JXSL XH TDOMO PUWVOR

XYPD HXW KNN.

UDJWDAO 10:10

Clue: O = S

103 Not Man's Best Friend

FEL TY GPRPIPM FMKT KZFCP SBP MTXL, KFVNEO, SBP

LTOK KBFMM PFS GPRPIPM IV SBP DFMM TY GPRXPPM.

1 CNEOK 21:23

Clue: L = D

MNG ENUD FBKS YNWABDDSE WS: PFS BDDSWICV NM

PFS ROYTSE FBKS OXYCNDSE WS: PFSV AOSGYSE WV

FBXED BXE WV MSSP.

ADBCW 22:16

Clue: Y = C

The Awesomeness of God, Part 1

DWV MY PWJ LXJYYJI KFI VFXT GVPJFPKPJ, PWJ QMFO

VZ QMFOY, KFI XVHI VZ XVHIY; DWV VFXT WKPW

MNNVHPKXMPT, IDJXXMFO MF PWJ XMOWP DWMRW

FV NKF RKF KGGHVKRW AFPV; DWVN FV NKF WKPW

YJJF, FVH RKF YJJ: PV DWVN LJ WVFVAH KFI GVDJH

JCJHXKYPMFO.

1 PMNVPWT 6:15—16   *Clue: G = P*

———————————

HNE AGJP PSMAG AGK GMBG SIV YNHAC NIK AGSA

MIGSXMAKAG KAKEIMAC, ZGNPK ISWK MP GNYC;

M VZKYY MI AGK GMBG SIV GNYC UYSRK, ZMAG

GMW SYPN AGSA MP NH S RNIAEMAK SIV GJWXYK

PUMEMA.

MPSMSG 57:15   *Clue: H = F*

105 The Awesomeness of God, Part 2

GCBU ILST S, EAB SI RB! MAN S LR OUTAUB; DBYLOIB S

LR L RLU AM OUYPBLU PSFI, LUT S TEBPP SU GCB RSTIG

AM L FBAFPB AM OUYPBLU PSFI: MAN RSUB BVBI CLJB

IBBU GCB QSUX, GCB PANT AM CAIGI.

SILSLC 6:5

Clue: O = U

L HB HJDKH HEW RBTMH, YKT NTMLEELEM HEW YKT

TEWLEM, IHLYK YKT JRPW, XKLVK LI, HEW XKLVK XHI,

HEW XKLVK LI YR VRBT, YKT HJBLMKYG.

PTQTJHYLRE 1:8

Clue: I = S

106 Scenes by the River

WZ CBFX SWPP UAC IFPWFEF NPJA CBFJF CSA JWLUJ,

UFWCBFH BFNHQFU GUCA CBX EAWTF, CBNC CBAG

JBNPC CNQF AZ CBF SNCFH AZ CBF HWEFH, NUM

DAGH WC GDAU CBF MHX PNUM: NUM CBF SNCFH

SBWTB CBAG CNQFJC AGC AZ CBF HWEFH JBNPP

IFTARF IPAAM GDAU CBF MHX PNUM.

FOAMGJ 4:9   *Clue: G = U*

ZBQQT, OG DOBD IBV ITDO DOGG QGFAMH SAZHBM,

DA IOAP DOAC QBZGVD ITDMGVV, QGOAJH, DOG

VBPG QBYDTXGDO, BMH BJJ PGM EAPG DA OTP.

SAOM BMVIGZGH BMH VBTH, B PBM EBM ZGEGTWG

MADOTML, GREGYD TD QG LTWGM OTP KZAP

OGBWGM.

SAOM 3:26–27   *Clue: S = J*

107 An Even Dozen

EKK HNRAR ECR HNR HPRKQR HCWVRA TM WACERK:

ESU HNWA WA WH HNEH HNRWC MEHNRC AYEOR

BSHT HNRD, ESU VKRAARU HNRD; RQRCJ TSR.

FRSRAWA 49:28

Clue: T = O

MXU HO AMQL OS CMII MGOLNEMNU, OYMO

YL ELXO OYNSTJYSTO LKLND AHOD MXU KHZZMJL,

CNLMAYHXJ MXU IYLEHXJ OYL JZMU OHUHXJI SG OYL

PHXJUSQ SG JSU: MXU OYL OELZKL ELNL EHOY YHQ.

ZTPL 8:1

Clue: E = W

108 *The Story of Zacchaeus*

MQE SF IVLJSA AV IFF BFILI YSV SF YMI; MQE RVLNE

QVA PVU ASF KUFII, ZFRMLIF SF YMI NWAANF VP

IAMALUF. MQE SF UMQ ZFPVUF, MQE RNWDZFE LK

WQAV M IXRVDVUF AUFF AV IFF SWD: PVU SF YMI AV

KMII ASMA YMX.

NLCF 19:3-4   *Clue: R = C*

———————————

DTG RLKZK KDNG ZTEW QNC, EQNK GDU NK

KDBYDENWT PWCL EW EQNK QWZKL, VWJKWCZPQ DK

QL DBKW NK D KWT WV DSJDQDC. VWJ EQL KWT WV

CDT NK PWCL EW KLLI DTG EW KDYL EQDE XQNPQ

XDK BWKE.

BZIL 19:9-10   *Clue: N = I*

109 · Moses' Sister

LHF STO WGPBF FOZLNSOF ANPC PAA STO

SLDONHLWGO; LHF, DOTPGF, CENELC DOWLCO

GOZNPBJ, ITESO LJ JHPI: LHF LLNPH GPPQOF BZPH

CENELC, LHF, DOTPGF, JTO ILJ GOZNPBJ.

HBCDONJ 12:10

Clue: J = S

PHN LCACPL MGY TAITGYMYKK, MGY KCKMYA IV PPAIH,

MIIF P MCLUAYZ CH GYA GPHN; PHN PZZ MGY DILYH

DYHM IJM PVMYA GYA DCMG MCLUAYZK PHN DCMG

NPHOYK. PHN LCACPL PHKDYAYN MGYL, KCHE SY MI

MGY ZIAN, VIA GY GPMG MACJLTGYN EZIACIJKZS.

YWINJK 15:20–21

Clue: D = W

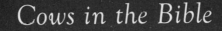

Cows in the Bible

SLC PXC GSCT HOT ITSWH XY HOT TSMHO SYHTM

OBW NBLC, SLC ASHHZT SYHTM HOTBM NBLC, SLC

TETMR HOBLP HOSH AMTTVTHO FVXL HOT TSMHO

SYHTM OBW NBLC: SLC PXC WSU HOSH BH USW PXXC.

PTLTWBW 1:25   *Clue: P = G*

CBU MOP HESU ROCHH ICVP MOPP QHPBMPETR NB

JEEUR, NB MOP YSTNM EY MOG KEUG, CBU NB MOP

YSTNM EY MOG ZCMMHP, CBU NB MOP YSTNM EY

MOG JSETBU, NB MOP HCBU FONZO MOP HESU

RFCSP TBME MOG YCMOPSR ME JNDP MOPP.

UPTMPSEBEIG 28:11   *Clue: H = L*

111 *Holy, Holy, Holy*

Y LYT, KMYE CZK KJZZVUQJ YEK YW KMR MYQR

NQCIJF: KMJ LYT YW VFZCJQ VF MJ KMCK LVPJKM

FKZJGLKM CGT NYDJZ EGKY MVF NJYNQJ. UQJFFJT UJ

LYT.

NFCQX 68:35   *Clue: Q = L*

IVM DBPV LBP TFOM NID LBIL BP LHOVPM INCMP LF

NPP, SFM AITTPM HVLF BCU FHL FG LBP UCMNL FG

LBP ZHNB, IVM NICM, UFNPN, UFNPN. IVM BP NICM,

BPOP IU C. IVM BP NICM, MOID VFL VCSB BCLBPO: XHL

FGG LBK NBFPN GOFU FGG LBK GPPL, GFO LBP XTIAP

DBPOPFV LBFH NLIVMPNL CN BFTK SOFHVM.

PYFMHN 3:4–5   *Clue: D = W*

Makin' Music

MLBXPDEV FW QWNOMBGABM DE LMXGTM XEC IQTEM

XEC MLDODFNXG MWEVM, MDEVDEV XEC TXPDEV

TBGWCQ DE QWNO IBXOF FW FIB GWOC; VDADEV

FIXEPM XGKXQM RWO XGG FIDEVM NEFW VWC.

BLIBMDXEM 5:19–20   *Clue: Q = Y*

LG SJY SQAOHYSYQG LMV GCMEYQG NYQY LG WMY,

SW OLPY WMY GWAMV SW ZY JYLQV CM HQLCGCME

LMV SJLMPCME SJY UWQV; LMV NJYM SJYK UCBSYV AH

SJYCQ RWCDY NCSJ SJY SQAOHYSG LMV DKOZLUG

LMV CMGSQAOYMSG WB OAGCDP, LMV HQLCGYV

SJY UWQV, GLKCME, BWQ JY CG EWWV; BWQ JCG

OYQDK YMVAQYSJ BWQ YRYQ: SJLS SJYM SJY JWAGY

NLG BCUUYV NCSJ L DUWAV.

2 DJQWMCDUYG 5:13   *Clue: O = M*

113 *Bones*

DRH LGWAW OGGP OIA TGRAW GX ZGWAUI EVOI IVL:

XGN IA IDH WONDVOMC WEGNR OIA SIVMHNAR GX

VWNDAM, WDCVRY, YGH EVMM WKNAMC BVWVO

CGK; DRH CA WIDMM SDNNC KU LC TGRAW DEDC

IARSA EVOI CGK.

AFGHKW 13:19

Clue: E = W

QCUG LKSHU, LMM QCU RLMWLTQ PUT, LTO QSSE

LALG QCU FSOG SX HLBM, LTO QCU FSOWUH SX

CWH HSTH, LTO FKSBVCQ QCUP QS NLFUHC, LTO

FBKWUO QCUWK FSTUH BTOUK QCU SLE WT NLFUHC,

LTO XLHQUO HURUT OLGH.

1 ZCKSTWZMUH 10:12

Clue: F = B.

From Psalm 119

AJLB KT DIMO BNRP J HPFDNVPH NDD LBP ZXHQKPELO

IG LBT KIXLB. J BNRP VPZIJFPH JE LBP ANT IG LBT

LPOLJKIEJPO, NO KXFB NO JE NDD VJFBPO. J AJDD

KPHJLNLP JE LBT MVPFPMLO, NEH BNRP VPOMPFL XELI

LBT ANTO.

MONDK 119:13–15   *Clue: K = M*

———————

VSWI CI PAYIEJNKAYSAV, KAY S JFKQQ ZIIH NFR QKO;

RIK, S JFKQQ ULJIEWI SN OSNF CR OFUQI FIKEN. CKZI

CI NU VU SA NFI HKNF UG NFR BUCCKAYCIANJ; GUE

NFIEISA YU S YIQSVFN.

HJKQC 119:34–35   *Clue: Y = D*

115 *More from Psalm 119*

NCI IMJNC, A BAJR, GF WXBB AW NCH DIJPH: NIMPC

DI NCH FNMNXNIF. NCAX CMFN RIMBN LIBB LGNC

NCH FIJTMSN, A BAJR, MPPAJRGSY XSNA NCH LAJR.

NIMPC DI YAAR KXRYDISN MSR QSALBIRYI: WAJ G CMTI

EIBGITIR NCH PADDMSRDISNF.

VFMBD 119:64–66   *Clue: P = C*

RMA PGUDAT MBYA EBGT B ZLBKA OIK CA: NAR G

AKKAT LIR OKIC RMN VKAUAVRZ. RMN RAZRGCILGAZ

MBYA G RBDAL BZ BL MAKGRBXA OIK AYAK: OIK

RMAN BKA RMA KAQIGUGLX IO CN MABKR. G MBYA

GLUEGLAT CGLA MABKR RI VAKOIKC RMN ZRBRSRAZ

BEPBN, AYAL SLRI RMA ALT.

VZBEC 119:110–112   *Clue: I = O*

116 *Giant Trouble*

SRE AGFZF MFRA UIA S LGSNKPUR UIA UY AGF LSNK

UY AGF KGPJPOAPRFO, RSNFE WUJPSAG, UY WSAG,

MGUOF GFPWGA MSO OPB LIQPAO SRE S OKSR.

1 OSNIFJ 17:4   *Clue: L = C*

KMH RFN KJKBM NDFPF CKV CKP KN JKND, CDFPF

CKV K OKM GA JPFKN VNKNEPF, CDGVF ABMJFPV

KMH NGFV CFPF AGEP KMH NCFMNR, VBW GM FKQD

DKMH, KMH VBW GM FKQD AGGN KMH DF KIVG CKV

NDF VGM GA NDF JBKMN.

1 QDPGMBQIFV 20:6   *Clue: J = G*

 117 New Testament Rulers

KNL LBMK PMZYZ LOZ GNTK UK GMWBQMBMF NS

PYHOMO UK WBM HOEZ NS BMTNH WBM DUKI,

GMBNQH, WBMTM ROFM LUZM FMK STNF WBM

MOZW WN PMTYZOQMF.

FOWWBML 2:1   *Clue: G = B*

———————

HTS NPCIC HTCQPVWTF CHWS ITOL OAPK, VPTSPV OL

ZHPCHV OAP OAWTFC OAHO HVP ZHPCHV'C, HTS OL

FLS OAP OAWTFC OAHO HVP FLS'C.

KHVB 12:17   *Clue: F = G*

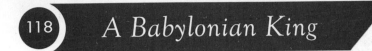

A Babylonian King

ROJS SJPTUOMISJWWMB ROJ FKSC LJSR RY CMROJB

RYCJROJB ROJ GBKSUJL, ROJ CYQJBSYBL, MSI ROJ

UMGRMKSL, ROJ ETICJL, ROJ RBJMLTBJBL, ROJ UYTSLJHHYBL,

ROJ LOJBKZZL, MSI MHH ROJ BTHJBL YZ ROJ GBYQKSUJL,

RY UYVJ RY ROJ IJIKUMRKYS YZ ROJ KVMCJ DOKUO

SJPTUOMISJWWMB ROJ FKSC OMI LJR TG.

IMSKJH 3:2   *Clue: I = D*

_____

SXTC CTYPRXFWCTBBFK GZFLT, FCW GFAW, YUTGGTW

YT SXT DQW QM GXFWKFRX, ITGXFRX, FCW FYTWCTDQ,

VXQ XFSX GTCS XAG FCDTU, FCW WTUAHTKTW XAG

GTKHFCSG SXFS SKPGSTW AC XAI, FCW XFHT RXFCDTW

SXT LACD'G VQKW.

WFCATU 3:28   *Clue: D = G*

119 *Rules for Church Leaders*

J NGHFPT CFLE WKHC NL NZJWLZLHH, CFL FKHNJEV PX

PEL AGXL, IGYGZJEC, HPNLD, PX YPPV NLFJIGPKD, YGILE

CP FPHTGCJZGCR, JTC CP CLJOF; EPC YGILE CP AGEL, EP

HCDGBLD, EPC YDLLVR PX XGZCFR ZKODL; NKC TJCGLEC,

EPC J NDJAZLD, EPC OPILCPKH.

1 CGWPCFR 3:2–3   *Clue: D = R*

———————

DTMR DTM DGMIJM ZBIIMQ DTM LXIDUDXQM KW

DTM QUEZUSIME XRDK DTML, BRQ EBUQ, UD UE RKD

FMBEKR DTBD GM ETKXIQ IMBJM DTM GKFQ KW AKQ,

BRQ EMFJM DBPIME. GTMFMWKFM, PFMDTFMR, IKKC

OM KXD BLKRA OKX EMJMR LMR KW TKRMED FMSKFD,

WXII KW DTM TKIO ATKED BRQ GUEQKL.

BZDE 6:2–3   *Clue: Z = C*

120 Spiritual U-Turns

GEF SVNW NPYA, EG J CJMY, GEJNP NPY CWZO

UWO, J PEMY VW ICYEGSZY JV NPY OYENP WK NPY

DJLRYO; XSN NPEN NPY DJLRYO NSZV KZWA PJG DEF

EVO CJMY: NSZV FY, NSZV FY KZWA FWSZ YMJC DEFG;

KWZ DPF DJCC FY OJY, W PWSGY WK JGZEYC?

YBYRJYC 33:11   *Clue: C = L*

UXSQ, E PVIRMJWZWQA ITWJZSKQ, MVWUT UTK JESZ;

NES W VH HVSSWKZ XQUE BEX: VQZ W OWJJ UVRK

BEX EQK EN V IWUB, VQZ UOE EN V NVHWJB, VQZ

W OWJJ PSWQA BEX UE GWEQ.

YKSKHWVT 3:14   *Clue: E = O*

121 Hellish Stuff

YKO CG AUX UYKO NGGIKO AUII, PQA CA NGG: CA

CJ RIAAIV GNV AUII AN IKAIV CKAN TCGI SYCSIO,

AUYK UYWCKD AZN UYKOJ AN DN CKAN UITT, CKAN

AUI GCVI AUYA KIWIV JUYTT RI MQIKPUIO: ZUIVI AUICV

ZNVS OCIAU KNA, YKO AUI GCVI CJ KNA MQIKPUIO.

SYVB 9:43–44   *Clue: U = H*

UML EQP NPUAE TUA EUFPM, UML TBEQ QBD EQP

HUVAP IZXIQPE EQUE TZXWRQE DBZUSVPA NPHXZP

QBD, TBEQ TQBSQ QP LPSPBCPL EQPD EQUE QUL

ZPSPBCPL EQP DUZF XH EQP NPUAE, UML EQPD EQUE

TXZAQBIIPL QBA BDURP. EQPAP NXEQ TPZP SUAE UVBCP

BMEX U VUFP XH HBZP NWZMBMR TBEQ NZBDAEXMP.

ZPCPVUEBXM 19:20   *Clue: N = B*

More Hellish Stuff

GDA AMK TKCUTDB, CLJ DLGKBSKQSLV, CLJ AMK

CGXNSLCGBK, CLJ NDUJKUKUO, CLJ PMXUKNXLVKUO,

CLJ OXUIKUKUO, CLJ SJXBCAKUO, CLJ CBB BSCUO,

OMCBB MCQK AMKSU WCUA SL AMK BCEK PMSIM

GDULKAM PSAM TSUK CLJ GUSNOAXLK: PMSIM SO

AMK OKIXLJ JKCAM.

UKQKBCASXL 21:8   *Clue: P = W*

―――――――――――――

GIBQ AMUMOWG, CDMC DI EMJ QPZ CDI CPZ VL

DPG LPBRIO PB YMCIO, MBQ NVVA EJ CVBRWI; LVO

P ME CVOEIBCIQ PB CDPG LAMEI. TWC MTOMDME

GMPQ, GVB, OIEIETIO CDMC CDVW PB CDJ APLICPEI

OINIPFIQGC CDJ RVVQ CDPBRG, MBQ APHIYPGI

AMUMOWG IFPA CDPBRG: TWC BVY DI PG NVELVOCIQ,

MBQ CDVW MOC CVOEIBCIQ.

AWHI 16:24―25   *Clue: L = F*

123 *Heavenly Stuff*

ZSI AO PZTI LSQU NOPLP, EUJI, JORORXOJ RO HAOS

QAUL VUROPQ TSQU QAW DTSFIUR. ZSI NOPLP PZTI

LSQU ATR, MOJTEW T PZW LSQU QAOO, QUIZW

PAZEQ QAUL XO HTQA RO TS GZJZITPO.

ELDO 23:42–43

Clue: I = D

———————

PWV O UWNQ ITGA P EPW, (QANJANH OW JAN

YDVL, DH DTJ DS JAN YDVL, O GPWWDJ JNMM: FDV

UWDQNJA;) ADQ JAPJ AN QPI GPTFAJ TK OWJD

KPHPVOIN, PWV ANPHV TWIKNPUPYMN QDHVI, QAOGA

OJ OI WDJ MPQSTM SDH P EPW JD TJJNH.

2 GDHOWJAOPWI 12:3–4

Clue: T = U

124 More Heavenly Stuff

VPH GVTG DUZIMDHZGV JPFF P HTYZ T BPFFTI PX GVZ

GZHBFZ DK HS ODQ, TXQ VZ LVTFF OD XD HDIZ DCG:

TXQ P JPFF JIPGZ CBDX VPH GVZ XTHZ DK HS ODQ, TXQ

GVZ XTHZ DK GVZ MPGS DK HS ODQ, JVPMV PL XZJ

AZICLTFZH, JVPMV MDHZGV QDJX DCG DK VZTUZX KIDH

HS ODQ: TXQ P JPFF JIPGZ CBDX VPH HS XZJ XTHZ.

IZUZFTGPDX 3:12   *Clue: F = L*

_____

PWC CLKP GEE JLK AKWAEK CKVK XGAJSHKR, SJ NGDK

JW AGMM, JLGJ TKMZM GEMW XKSPI XGAJSHKR, GPR

AVGFSPI, JLK LKGBKP CGM WAKPKR, GPR JLK LWEF

ILWMJ RKMNKPRKR SP G XWRSEF MLGAK ESYK G RWBK

ZAWP LSD, GPR G BWSNK NGDK QVWD LKGBKP,

CLSNL MGSR, JLWZ GVJ DF XKEWBKR MWP.

EZYK 3:21–22   *Clue: C = W*

125 *Lesser–Known Disciples*

GRENF FNCOI RDOT ICW, DTO CFUNHCTO, ATHE, ITM

CF CO OINO OITR MCAO WNDCLKFO OIXFKAL RDOT

RF, NDE DTO RDOT OIK MTHAE?

GTID 14:22

Clue: F = S

———————

MS XWQS IULAP XOG, UI MXUG GUDSD OA YXS

HWM, WAP YXS JZUJXSYD, POP MZOYS, VSDLD UI

AWKWZSYX, YXS DUA UI VUDSJX. WAP AWYXWAWSH

DWOP LAYU XOG, FWA YXSZS WAT NUUP YXOAN

FUGS ULY UI AWKWZSYX? JXOHOJ DWOYX LAYU XOG,

FUGS WAP DSS.

VUXA 1:45–46

Clue: J = P

Biblical Horses

SWA EXU XWARU WS MXOAOWX IUPE ZP IZEX XZR

KXOAZWER OPN IZEX XZR XWARUBUP ZPEW EXU RUO,

OPN EXU GWAN CAWYHXE OHOZP EXU IOEUAR WS

EXU RUO YMWP EXUB; CYE EXU KXZGNAUP WS ZRAOUG

IUPE WP NAQ GOPN ZP EXU BZNRE WS EXU RUO.

UVWNYR 15:19 *Clue: N = D*

KMY MXVZLN BPLL KM KNVR, UJHL BPL KNVR BPKB BPFX

PKQB UFQB, PFNQL CFN PFNQL, KMY TPKNJFB CFN

TPKNJFB: KMY DL DJUU CJOPB KOKJMQB BPLV JM BPL

IUKJM, KMY QXNLUR DL QPKUU ZL QBNFMOLN BPKM

BPLR. KMY PL PLKNHLMLY XMBF BPLJN AFJTL, KMY YJY

QF.

1 HJMOQ 20:25 *Clue: J = I*

Villains

IBVZIMPVG OLV NRQQVGAKHOL PHP KV KCNL VXHB:

OLV BRGP GVDIGP LHK INNRGPHMW OR LHA DRGSA:

RE DLRK TV OLRC DIGV IBAR; ERG LV LIOL WGVIOBU

DHOLAORRP RCG DRGPA.

2 OHKROLU 4:14–15   *Clue: P = D*

_____

NFM UW HUGBQUH ROGDF HG JNP UNFMR GF

KGDMWONS NJGFW; IGD HUWP UNM RUWAWM USK

HUW LWGLJW GI KGDMWONS: AUWDWIGDW UNKNF

RGBQUH HG MWRHDGP NJJ HUW YWAR HUNH

AWDW HUDGBQUGBH HUW AUGJW TSFQMGK GI

NUNRBWDBR, WXWF HUW LWGLJW GI KGDMWONS.

WRHUWD 3:6   *Clue: R = S*

Noah's Ark

NTC EZQU QU EZB XNUZQPT JZQHZ EZPI UZNFE

DNWB QE PX: EZB FBTLEZ PX EZB NOW UZNFF RB

EZOBB ZITCOBC HIRQEU, EZB ROBNCEZ PX QE XQXEV

HIRQEU, NTC EZB ZBQLZE PX QE EZQOEV HIRQEU.

LBTBUQU 6:15   *Clue: T = N*

DVJFJ PJGD SG DPE BGX DPE RGDE GEBV SGDE DVJ

BFH, DVJ LBYJ BGX DVJ UJLBYJ, BC KEX VBX NELLBGXJX

GEBV.

KJGJCSC 7:9   *Clue: L = M*

Executions

VBI XCT, RTEBS RTWDNT EBXJNFLJTI DW CTN ODJCTN,

XVEI, SEPT OT CTNT UDCB RVYJEXJ'X CTVI EB V

LCVNSTN.

OVJJCTZ 14:8

Clue: V = A

UY ALJB LHIXJZ LHEHI YI ALJ XHFFYPU ALHA LJ LHZ

ODJOHDJZ SYD EYDZJTHC. ALJI PHU ALJ QCIX'U PDHAL

OHTCSCJZ.

JUALJD 7:10

Clue: H = A

130   *Fish Fry*

CLGTG FG TLZJJ GZC KX ZJJ CLZC ZMG PS CLG

UZCGMT: ZJJ CLZC LZIG XPST ZSV TBZJGT TLZJJ FG GZC.

VGECGMKSYF 14:9   *Clue: J = L*

KM MGGI JLWI KM JLWF BWZW YGAW JG PKIX, JLWF

MKB K CUZW GC YGKPM JLWZW, KIX CUML PKUX

JLWZWGI, KIX TZWKX.

NGLI 21:9   *Clue: W = E*

131 *Planting and Harvesting*

FSCU SJRC VQNA NSCJF, LXF VSJWW GCJE FSQGAV:

FSCU SJRC EXF FSCTVCWRCV FQ EJOA, LXF VSJWW

AQF EGQHOF: JAY FSCU VSJWW LC JVSJTCY QH UQXG

GCRCAXCV LCDJXVC QH FSC HOCGDC JAKCG QH FSC

WQGY.

BCGCTOJS 12:13

Clue: T = M

QD FAC ODJDMTDO; VAO MP FAC SAJIDO: RAE

BNKCPADTDE K SKF PABDCN, CNKC PNKYY ND KYPA

EDKG. RAE ND CNKC PABDCN CA NMP RYDPN PNKYY

AR CND RYDPN EDKG JAEEXGCMAF; QXC ND CNKC

PABDCN CA CND PGMEMC PNKYY AR CND PGMEMC

EDKG YMRD DTDEYKPCMFV.

VKYKCMKFP 6:7–8

Clue: P = S

132 · *Other Farm Analogies*

QYKOB AUE SO SE YSO YUEJ, UEJ YB QSZZ FYTKGXYZL

WGTXB YSO AZKKT, UEJ XUFYBT YSO QYBUF SEFK FYB

XUTEBT; DGF YB QSZZ DGTE GW FYB MYUAA QSFY

GEIGBEMYUDZB ASTB.

RUFFYBQ 3:12   *Clue: Q = W*

_____

MYI OC BZ IGC DBJFWC, LPS IGC GNSUCDI BD SBMC:

JPVC, RCI OPY QPEZ; LPS IGC MSCDD BD LYWW, IGC

LNID PUCSLWPE; LPS IGCBS EBJFCQZCDD BD RSCNI.

TPCW 3:13   *Clue: S = R*

133) *Athletics in the Bible*

B IQVTVSFTV JF TDR, RFI YJ DRKVTIYBRWH; JF SBXQI B,

RFI YJ FRV IQYI MVYIVIQ IQV YBT: MDI B CVVU DREVT

GH MFEH, YRE MTBRX BI BRIF JDMLVKIBFR: WVJI IQYI

MH YRH GVYRJ, NQVR B QYOV UTVYKQVE IF FIQVTJ, B

GHJVWS JQFDWE MV Y KYJIYNYH.

1 KFTBRIQBYRJ 9:26–27   *Clue: T = R*

AKRSRGLSR VRRUYJ AR IZVL ISR XLFCIVVRE IMLTO AUOK

VL JSRIO I XZLTE LG AUOYRVVRV, ZRO TV ZIB IVUER

RNRSB ARUJKO, IYE OKR VUY AKUXK ELOK VL RIVUZB

MRVRO TV, IYE ZRO TV STY AUOK CIOURYXR OKR SIXR

OKIO UV VRO MRGLSR TV.

KRMSRAV 12:1   *Clue: X = C*

Weaponry

UZA KXC PDMA YUOA EZKD BDYXEU, YKMCKWX DEK

KXC YICUM KXUK OY OZ KXH XUZA KDNUMA UO;

GDM O NOPP JOFC OK OZKD KXOZC XUZA. UZA

BDYXEU YKMCKWXCA DEK KXC YICUM KXUK XC XUA

OZ XOY XUZA KDNUMA KXC WOKH.

BDYXEU 8:18   *Clue: U = A*

HDURT BOOUHR BOT RDBOZ, BJI BXX GDTLO SUHR

STJG, GDTLO DUORTR' DUUYR RDBXX ST FUPJGTI XLCT

YXLJG, BJI GDTLO HDTTXR XLCT B HDLOXHLJI.

LRBLBD 5:28   *Clue: H = W*

135 *How Big Is God?*

WF P W MXZ WS KWRZ, NWPSK SKV EXJZ, WRZ RXS

W MXZ WTWJ XTT? IWR WRO KPZV KPFNVET PR NVIJVS

QEWIVN SKWS P NKWEE RXS NVV KPF? NWPSK SKV

EXJZ. ZX RXS P TPEE KVWBVR WRZ VWJSK? NWPSK SKV

EXJZ.

YVJVFPWK 23:23–24   *Clue: K = H*

NKHCKPD LKSUU H XW BDWE CKF LOHDHC? WD

NKHCKPD LKSUU H BUPP BDWE CKF ODPLPVTP? HB H

SLTPVI MO HVCW KPSRPV, CKWM SDC CKPDP: HB H

ESJP EF QPI HV KPUU, QPKWUI, CKWM SDC CKPDP.

OLSUE 139:7–8   *Clue: L = S*

136 · *Biblical Kisses*

XPUTN EJW IUMIK EUP XPI IDAPIKPU; UHAKIPDMQJPQQ

EJW BPETP KESP OHQQPW PETK DIKPU.

BQEZX 85:10

Clue: E = A

EIXU WBVQM LBE OBVIXC HIX TBDPIHXO QR CBMBU

IKL AQHIXO'L MOQHIXO, BUT HIX LIXXS QR CBMBU

IKL AQHIXO'L MOQHIXO, HIBH WBVQM EXUH UXBO,

BUT OQCCXT HIX LHQUX ROQA HIX EXCC'L AQDHI,

BUT EBHXOXT HIX RCQVG QR CBMBU IKL AQHIXO'L

MOQHIXO. BUT WBVQM GKLLXT OBVIXC.

PXUXLKL 29:10–11

Clue: M = B

137 Honesty Is the Best Policy

J SJWCR IJWJBFR OC JITHOBJGOTB GT GAR WTUY: IQG

J NQCG XROVAG OC AOC YRWOVAG.

LUTMRUIC 11:1

Clue: R = E

PVR DEPD TO GFD ZV DEO VOI UPV, IEYME PQDOW

LZR YA MWOPDOR YV WYLEDOZFAVOAA PVR DWFO

EZXYVOAA. IEOWOQZWO GFDDYVL PIPT XTYVL, AGOPJ

OSOWT UPV DWFDE IYDE EYA VOYLEKZFW: QZW IO

PWO UOUKOWA ZVO ZQ PVZDEOW.

OGEOAYPVA 4:24–25

Clue: G = P

Battle Scenes

VPI DSB KUNI IBKEZBNBI ED VKTU, VPI DSB REPF DSBNBUA,

EPDU DSB SVPI UA ETNVBK; VPI SB TYUDB ED GEDS DSB BIFB

UA DSB TGUNI, VPI VKK DSB TUOKT DSVD GBNB DSBNBEP;

SB KBD PUPB NBYVEP EP ED; XOD IEI OPDU DSB REPF

DSBNBUA VT SB IEI OPDU DSB REPF UA LBNEWSU.

LUTSOV 10:30   *Clue: K = L*

NBD EHYKZ RFAD FYX WLJKBN, NBDY WLJKBN NBD

EHYKZ LW RFYFFY HY NFFYFRB SG NBD QFNDUZ LW

ADKHXXL; NBDG NLLO YL KFHY LW ALYDG. NBDG

WLJKBN WULA BDFMDY; NBD ZNFUZ HY NBDHU

RLJUZDZ WLJKBN FKFHYZN ZHZDUF.

IJXKDZ 5:19–20   *Clue: Y = N*

139 *Ancient Places*

UPC LI RUOC TPVN LOA, O UA VLI KNGC VLUV

HGNTBLV VLII NTV NY TG NY VLI ZLUKCIIR, VN BOMI

VLII VLOR KUPC VN OPLIGOV OV.

BIPIROR 15:7

Clue: C = D

XAPEP CMF M SMI YI XAP WMIU DV LK, CADFP IMSP

CMF GDO; MIU XAMX SMI CMF BPEVPZX MIU LBEYHAX,

MIU DIP XAMX VPMEPU HDU, MIU PFZAPCPU PQYW.

GDO 1:1

Clue: D = O

Crazy, Man

NBG GNKLG CNLG TQ RPWXW DJHGX LB PLX PWNHR,

NBG DNX XJHW NSHNLG JS NVPLXP RPW MLBI JS

INRP. NBG PW VPNBIWG PLX ZWPNKLJTH ZWSJHW RPWO,

NBG SWLIBWG PLOXWCS ONG LB RPWLH PNBGX, NBG

XVHNZZCWG JB RPW GJJHX JS RPW INRW, NBG CWR

PLX XQLRRCW SNCC GJDB TQJB PLX ZWNHG.

1 XNOTWC 21:12–13   *Clue: I = G*

————————

WUJPQJ JMVO LVPN M AGQO KGVHU, SMQA, PNGQ

MBP IUJVOU PNTJUAW; XQHN AUMBZVZD OGPN XMFU

PNUU XMO. IQP NU JMVO, V MX ZGP XMO, XGJP

ZGIAU WUJPQJ; IQP JSUMF WGBPN PNU LGBOJ GW

PBQPN MZO JGIUBZUJJ.

MHPJ 26:24–25   *Clue: M = A*

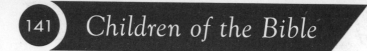

141 Children of the Bible

UYZ YED, BOFFBH WJOBZCHY, UAOZH OY JOT; FJUF,

DJHY JH RJUBB UIIHUC, DH TUK JUSH WEYMOZHYWH,

UYZ YEF AH URJUTHZ AHMECH JOT UF JOR WETOYQ.

1 LEJY 2:28   *Clue: Y = N*

_____

FTAD BAOA FTAOA ROIQLTF QDFI TGV PGFFPA

JTGPUOAD, FTSF TA NTIQPU HQF TGN TSDUN ID FTAV,

SDU HOSX: SDU FTA UGNJGHPAN OARQWAU FTAV.

RQF YANQN NSGU, NQZZAO PGFFPA JTGPUOAD, SDU

ZIORGU FTAV DIF, FI JIVA QDFI VA: ZIO IZ NQJT GN

FTA WGDLUIV IZ TASMAD.

VSFFTAB 19:13–14   *Clue: Z = F*

It's Magic

OKWVW NKTQQ PGO XW AGZPU TCGPM RGZ TPR

GPW OKTO CTLWOK KSN NGP GV KSN UTZMKOWV

OG FTNN OKVGZMK OKW ASVW, GV OKTO ZNWOK

USDSPTOSGP, GV TP GXNWVDWV GA OSCWN, GV TP

WPEKTPOWV, GV T JSOEK.

UWZOWVGPGCR 18:10   *Clue: K = H*

_____

I NIZ IMUS SC XSNIZ OTIO TIOT I VINJMJIC UGJCJO,

SC OTIO JU I XJDICQ, UTIMM URCPMK FP GRO OS

QPIOT: OTPK UTIMM UOSZP OTPN XJOT UOSZPU: OTPJC

FMSSQ UTIMM FP RGSZ OTPN.

MPAJOJHRU 20:27   *Clue: X = W*

143 Craftsmanship

VPSBAM TA HFA OCG HFCH OCZAHF CGQ NSCJAG

DS ODIHAG KOCNA, CG CTDOKGCHKDG PGHD HFA

IDSM, HFA XDSZ DY HFA FCGMB DY HFA VSCYHBOCG,

CGM EPHHAHF KH KG C BAVSAH EICVA. CGM CII HFA

EADEIA BFCII CGBXAS CGM BCQ, COAG.

MAPHASDGDOQ 27:15

Clue: P =U

EDH NUL KFCTL FY UEGJLGB, EDH AVBCTCEDB, EDH FY

JCJLGB, EDH NGVAJLNLGB, BUEZZ XL ULEGH DF AFGL

EN EZZ CD NULL; EDH DF TGEYNBAED, FY OUENBFLKLG

TGEYN UL XL, BUEZZ XL YFVDH EDR AFGL CD NULL; EDH

NUL BFVDH FY E ACZZBNFDL BUEZZ XL ULEGH DF AFGL

EN EZZ CD NULL.

GLKLZENCFD 18:22

Clue: X = B

God's Love

MUN YSKP YK YKNK HKJ YEJSUQJ AJNKPFJS, EP GQK
JELK BSNEAJ GEKG MUN JSK QPFUGDH.

NULTPA 5:6

Clue: Y = W

RUE A IV MBEZYITBT, QJIQ DBAQJBE TBIQJ, DUE SARB,
DUE IDLBSZ, DUE MEADGAMISAQABZ, DUE MUFBEZ,
DUE QJADLZ MEBZBDQ, DUE QJADLZ QU GUVB, DUE
JBALJQ, DUE TBMQJ, DUE IDH UQJBE GEBIQYEB, ZJISS
OB IOSB QU ZBMIEIQB YZ REUV QJB SUXB UR LUT,
FJAGJ AZ AD GJEAZQ NBZYZ UYE SUET.

EUVIDZ 8:38–39

Clue: M = P

145 On the Vine

WNCKQ CM SQ, WMK C CM IHY. WB EAQ NUWMFA

FWMMHE NQWU VUYCE HV CEBQZV, QJFQLE CE

WNCKQ CM EAQ DCMQ; MH SHUQ FWM IQ, QJFQLE

IQ WNCKQ CM SQ.

RHAM 15:4

Clue: W = A

LPK QFR LKMBQ PL QFR AIBKBQ BA BO ECC SPPYORAA

EOY KBSFQRPMAORAA EOY QKMQF; IKPJBOS XFEQ BA

EDDRIQETCR MOQP QFR CPKY.

RIFRABEOA 5:9–10

Clue: Q = T

146 *Jesus Describes Himself*

HSML WXYUM GMWIW YJYOL ILHE HSMR, WYCOLJ, O

YR HSM VOJSH ED HSM BEKVN: SM HSYH DEVVEBMHS

RM WSYVV LEH BYVU OL NYKULMWW, ZIH WSYVV

SYPM HSM VOJSH ED VODM.

GESL 8:12   *Clue: V = L*

———————

B DO IVS TUUQ: JP OS BC DGP ODG SGISQ BG, VS

HVDKK JS HDAST, DGT HVDKK YU BG DGT UXI, DGT

CBGT WDHIXQS. IVS IVBSC ZUOSIV GUI, JXI CUQ IU

HISDK, DGT IU RBKK, DGT IU TSHIQUP: B DO ZUOS

IVDI IVSP OBYVI VDAS KBCS, DGT IVDI IVSP OBYVI VDAS

BI OUQS DJXGTDGIKP.

NUVG 10:9–10   *Clue: B = I*

147 Paul Describes Himself

XN SJUNH LMP UC PXN SLMCSUO, WNC TCH

RJNPXJNC, U TW T KXTJUINN, PXN ILC LD T KXTJUINN:

LD PXN XLKN TCH JNIMJJNSPULC LD PXN HNTH U TW

STOONH UC AMNIPULC.

TSPI 23:6

Clue: K = P

RGSRNHRGYKX PVK KGFVPV XJT, ID PVK YPIRA ID

GYSJKE, ID PVK PSGZK ID ZKCUJHGC, JC VKZSKL ID

PVK VKZSKLY; JY PINRVGCF PVK EJL, J QVJSGYKK;

RICRKSCGCF MKJE, QKSYKRNPGCF PVK RVNSRV;

PINRVGCF PVK SGFVPKINYCKYY LVGRV GY GC PVK EJL,

ZEJHKEKYY.

QVGEGQQGJCY 3:5–6

Clue: P = T

I'm Depressed

BJK RL NBYH LC IBOO, GDHJ LDH OTJ KRK BZROH,

LDBL SCK IZHIBZHK B MHDHYHJL HBOL GRJK; BJK LDH

OTJ PHBL TICJ LDH DHBK CA FCJBD, LDBL DH ABRJLHK,

BJK GRODHK RJ DRYOHUA LC KRH, BJK OBRK, RL RO

PHLLHZ ACZ YH LC KRH LDBJ LC URMH.

FCJBD   4:8   *Clue: O = S*

QZV AB AUIPBJE KBSV H YHT'P RNZCSBT USVN VAB

KUJYBCSBPP, HSY WHIB HSY PHV YNKS ZSYBC H

RZSUMBC VCBB: HSY AB CBOZPBVBY ENC AUIPBJE

VAHV AB IUFAV YUB; HSY PHUY, UV UP BSNZFA; SNK,

N JNCY, VHXB HKHT IT JUEB; ENC U HI SNV QBVVBC

VAHS IT EHVABCP.

1 XUSFP 19:4   *Clue: A = H*

149   *I'm Full of Joy*

O ZOBB CBGPP XAG BEYI DX DBB XOWGP: AOP

RYDOPG PADBB SELXOLKDBBV CG OL WV WEKXA. WV

PEKB PADBB WDNG AGY CEDPX OL XAG BEYI: XAG

AKWCBG PADBB AGDY XAGYGEM, DLI CG FBDI.

RPDBW 34:1–2   *Clue: W = M*

———————

GOA FGLJ RGTA, FJ RHNB AHIU FGSOTEJ IUW BHLA,

GOA FJ RMTLTI UGIU LWXHTQWA TO SHA FJ RGYTHNL.

EHL UW UGIU LWSGLAWA IUW BHD WRIGIW HE UTR

UGOAFGTAWO: EHL, PWUHBA, ELHF UWOQWEHLIU GBB

SWOWLGITHOR RUGBB QGBB FW PBWRRWA.

BNCW 1:46–48   *Clue: A = D*

150 · *Solar Occurrences*

USG REB FQS FRCCG FRZNN, USG REB HCCS FRUKBG,

QSRZN REB ABCANB EUG UJBSOBG REBHFBNJBF QACS

REBZD BSBHZBF. ZF SCR REZF MDZRRBS ZS REB XCCT

CY PUFEBD? FC REB FQS FRCCG FRZNN ZS REB HZGFR

CY EBUJBS.

PCFEQU 10:13   *Clue: S = N*

KIL GM OKQ KVTDM MNJ QGZMN NTDH, KIL MNJHJ

OKQ K LKHFIJQQ TSJH KXX MNJ JKHMN DIMGX MNJ

IGIMN NTDH. KIL MNJ QDI OKQ LKHFJIJL, KIL MNJ

SJGX TW MNJ MJBYXJ OKQ HJIM GI MNJ BGLQM.

KIL ONJI PJQDQ NKL EHGJL OGMN K XTDL STGEJ,

NJ QKGL, WKMNJH, GIMT MNC NKILQ G ETBBJIL BC

QYGHGM.

XDFJ 23:44–46   *Clue: L = D*

Bible Cryptograms

151 — *Let's Party*

CAW PGSA HGSES WCTE PSQS SYVJQSW, HGS NJAR

LCWS C OSCEH FAHD CKK HGS VSDVKS HGCH PSQS

VQSESAH JA EGFEGCA HGS VCKCZS, XDHG FAHD

RQSCH CAW ELCKK, ESUSA WCTE, JA HGS ZDFQH DO

HGS RCQWSA DO HGS NJAR'E VCKCZS.

SEHGSQ 1:5

Clue: R = G

_____

TSYC HSXE IMUYDH M BOCCYL XL M DEFFYL, PMVV

CXH HSG JLOYCBD, CXL HSG RLYHSLYC, CYOHSYL HSG

UOCDIYC, CXL HSG LOPS CYOQSRXELD; VYDH HSYG

MVDX ROB HSYY MQMOC, MCB M LYPXIFYCPY RY IMBY

HSYY. REH TSYC HSXE IMUYDH M JYMDH, PMVV HSY

FXXL, HSY IMOIYB, HSY VMIY, HSY RVOCB: MCB HSXE

DSMVH RY RVYDDYB.

VEUY 14:12–14

Clue: V = L

152 Protected

EPR UMQPE MW OCY WLRUE, EPR BCN MW CE

PCUB: KRE IW EPRYROZYR DCWE ZOO EPR GZYVW

ZO BCYVURWW, CUB KRE IW LIE ZU EPR CYXZIY ZO

KMQPE.

YZXCUW 13:12   *Clue: Y = R*

LZC UM COA YOUPA SDVUZD UN EUI, COSC HA VSH

GA SGPA CU BCSMI SESKMBC COA YKPAB UN COA

IARKP. NUD YA YDABCPA MUC SESKMBC NPABO SMI

GPUUI, GZC SESKMBC LDKMXKLSPKCKAB, SESKMBC

LUYADB, SESKMBC COA DZPADB UN COA ISDQMABB

UN COKB YUDPI, SESKMBC BLKDKCZSP YKXQAIMABB

KM OKEO LPSXAB.

ALOABKSMB 6:11—12   *Clue: L = P*

153 Famous Names

QO VUSZB UQLUBUG, DBFP BF DUT XUAAFY ZJ MJ JRZ

SPZJ U CAUXF DBSXB BF TBJRAY UVZFL LFXFSWF VJL UP

SPBFLSZUPXF, JQFOFY; UPY BF DFPZ JRZ, PJZ IPJDSPM

DBSZBFL BF DFPZ.

BFQLFDT 11:8

Clue: S = I

AWOI VOIA YPIX EQUPE PI, QIE LQA COJDFO AWO

BDFE, QIE WO LQPE, VWD QR P, D BDFE XDE? QIE

VWQA PL RG WDNLO, AWQA AWDN WQLA CFDNXWA

RO WPAWOFAD?

2 LQRNOB 7:18

Clue: E = D

154) *More Famous Names*

EWG ITWV OYHPYW OCEHH FS FHSOOSG, EWG JCS

JCZYWS YU GENTG OCEHH FS SOJEFHTOCSG FSUYZS

JCS HYZG UYZ SNSZ.

1 ITWVO 2:45   *Clue: H = L*

———————

YESL IWLKYEKL KLC CKHNC VKCS K PWHSLKLY, JSPKFTS

ES BWHSC ENV KT ENT WRL TWFB.

1 TKVFSB 18:3   *Clue: E = H*

155 The Temptation of Christ

JUK ERHAH SRXUL OANN GO DVR VGNT LVGHD

IRDAIURK OIGB EGIKJU, JUK QJH NRK ST DVR HMXIXD

XUDG DVR QXNKRIURHH, SRXUL OGIDT KJTH DRBMDRK

GO DVR KRYXN. JUK XU DVGHR KJTH VR KXK RJD

UGDVXUL.

NACR 4:1–2   *Clue: Q = W*

———————————

WOO RETD XAYLU YTOO T BTKL RELL, WMH REL BOAUQ

AV RELF: VAU REWR TD HLOTKLULH IMRA FL; WMH RA

YEAFDALKLU T YTOO T BTKL TR. TV REAI RELULVAUL YTOR

YAUDETX FL, WOO DEWOO NL RETML. WMH CLDID

WMDYLULH WMH DWTH IMRA ETF, BLR RELL NLETMH FL,

DWRWM: VAU TR TD YUTRRLM, REAI DEWOR YAUDETX

REL OAUH REQ BAH.

OIPL 4:6–8   *Clue: H = D*

The Avenger

JS HR ORZSWCRJI XRWCRTWPR TWK GRPSHLRWPR;

JIRQG MSSJ YITZZ YZQKR QW KFR JQHR: MSG JIR KTN

SM JIRQG PTZTHQJN QY TJ ITWK, TWK JIR JIQWCY JITJ

YITZZ PSHR FLSW JIRH HTAR ITYJR.

KRFJRGSWSHN 32:35   *Clue: T = A*

DYP VU VEOJ VEYV YTO UH Y HOYTHFN EOYTV, GO

DVTUIL, HOYT IUV: GOEUNB, PUFT LUB ZANN XUJO

ZAVE MOILOYIXO, OMOI LUB ZAVE Y TOXUJQOIXO; EO

ZANN XUJO YIB DYMO PUF.

ADYAYE 35:4   *Clue: A = I*

157   *Valuables*

TFM CRV FW DLQ VLFQBHCYHB MQHRBFQHB US

GHRYHS, NGHQH SHUMGHQ ZLMG SLQ QFBM KLMG

JLQQFWM, RSK NGHQH MGUHYHB KL SLM TQHRP

MGQLFOG SLQ BMHRC: DLQ NGHQH VLFQ MQHRBFQH

UB, MGHQH NUCC VLFQ GHRQM TH RCBL.

ZRMMGHN 6:20–21   *Clue: C = L*

———————————

AEI FVH MPNH ETIV UNR, IUVE ZVVD, IUNM TNFUI IUC

MVED MUPDD AG SGKENSGH VZ IUGG: IUGT YUVMG

MUPDD IUVMG IUNTFM AG, YUNQU IUVE UPMI

BSVXNHGH? MV NM UG IUPI DPCGIU EB ISGPMESG

ZVS UNRMGDZ, PTH NM TVI SNQU IVYPSH FVH.

DELG 12:20–21   *Clue: S = R*

158 — Dazed and Confused

GJL NSPT RPOP GEE GQGXPL, ZJWAQBYS NSGN NSPT

KBPWNZAJPL GQAJD NSPQWPEMPW, WGTZJD, RSGN

NSZJD ZW NSZW? RSGN JPR LAYNOZJP ZW NSZW?

UAO RZNS GBNSAOZNT YAQQGJLPNS SP PMPJ NSP

BJYEPGJ WFZOZNW, GJL NSPT LA ACPT SZQ.

QGOI 1:27   *Clue: G = A*

NTA JKHNDNKPA XGJA NRUANTAV, GEP LAVA

XRECRKEPAP, SAXGKYA NTGN AQAVM JGE TAGVP NTAJ

YZAGO DE TDY RLE HGEUKGUA. GEP NTAM LAVA

GHH GJGBAP GEP JGVQAHHAP, YGMDEU REA NR

GERNTAV, SATRHP, GVA ERN GHH NTAYA LTDXT YZAGO

UGHDHGAGEY? GEP TRL TAGV LA AQAVM JGE DE RKV

RLE NREUKA?

GXNY 2:6–8   *Clue: P = D*

159 The Shepherd

GNV EFSP FS TDE VFS CNYVUVNLST, FS EDT CAKSL

EUVF BACHDTTUAP AP VFSC, GSBDNTS VFSJ MDUPVSL,

DPL ESZS TBDVVSZSL DGZADL, DT TFSSH FDKUPO PA

TFSHFSZL.

CDVVFSE 9:36   *Clue: A = O*

———————

H TN ABG XLLK WBGEBGUK, TSK CSLF NR WBGGE, TSK

TN CSLFS LP NHSG. TW ABG PTABGU CSLFGAB NG,

GQGS WL CSLF H ABG PTABGU: TSK H ZTR KLFS NR

ZHPG PLU ABG WBGGE.

YLBS 10:14–15   *Clue: N = M*

160 Fruit of the Vine

MI YIC MDLYO KLYP YID BCDIYE MDLYO, CUIX,

YID CUW BIYB KLCU CUPP, KUPY WP EI LYCI CUP

CGHPDYGTFP IS CUP TIYEDPEGCLIY, FPBC WP MLP: LC

BUGFF HP G BCGCXCP SID PJPD CUDIXEUIXC WIXD

EPYPDGCLIYB.

FPJLCLTXB 10:9   *Clue: E = G*

EWRMJEW, T XEPL LJY, MJ MIWD, WSWU MITR BPL,

MIWTE KPUBR, MIWTE STUWLPEBR, MIWTE JKTSWLPEBR,

PUB MIWTE IJYRWR, PKRJ MIW IYUBEWBMI XPEM JV

MIW DJUWL, PUB JV MIW ZJEU, MIW QTUW, PUB MIW

JTK, MIPM LW WGPZM JV MIWD.

UWIWDTPI 5:11   *Clue: R = S*

Love Songs

NU MLD NSSOD MJDD NECPT MLD MJDDU CG MLD

VCCA, UC KU EX QDOCYDA NECPT MLD UCPU. K UNM

ACVP WPADJ LKU ULNACV VKML TJDNM ADOKTLM, NPA

LKU GJWKM VNU UVDDM MC EX MNUMD.

UCPT CG UCOCECP 2:3   *Clue: V = W*

FXY KCQO QP JFB HXLT, UB PQPJTO, UB PMXZPT! FXY

UZGF STJJTO QP JFB HXLT JFCA YQAT! CAW JFT PUTHH

XK JFQAT XQAJUTAJP JFCA CHH PMQGTP!

PXAR XK PXHXUXA 4:10   *Clue: J = T*

162   *Introducing Peter's Brother*

NYR MPGLG, ONHJAYD KB UIP GPN SC DNHAHPP,

GNO UOS KQPUIQPY, GAXSY FNHHPR WPUPQ, NYR

NYRQPO IAG KQSUIPQ, FNGUAYD N YPU AYUS UIP

GPN: CSQ UIPB OPQP CAGIPQG.

XNUUIPO 4:18

Clue: A = I

DAB DI LRC KRCQRSFBC, TAKUBH, CRYDA SBVBU'C

JUDVLBU, CTRVL MAVD LRY, VLBUB RC T FTK LBUB, HLRQL

LTVL IROB JTUFBG FDTOBC, TAK VHD CYTFF IRCLBC: JMV

HLTV TUB VLBG TYDAP CD YTAG?

XDLA 6:8–9

Clue: D = O

163 Mysteries

FRJMJ VJ FRMJJ FRDAQZ TRDLR IMJ FEE TEAHJMSXG SEM

PJ, WJI, SEXM TRDLR D UAET AEF: FRJ TIW ES IA JIQGJ

DA FRJ IDM; FRJ TIW ES I ZJMCJAF XCEA I MELU; FRJ

TIW ES I ZRDC DA FRJ PDHZF ES FRJ ZJI; IAH FRJ TIW

ES I PIA TDFR I PIDH.

CMEBJMVZ 30:18–19

Clue: T = W

DJAGPO, C TAJR BGH F KBTSJIB; RJ TAFPP VGS FPP TPJJL,

DHS RJ TAFPP FPP DJ WAFVYJO, CV F KGKJVS, CV SAJ

SRCVEPCVY GM FV JBJ, FS SAJ PFTS SIHKL: MGI SAJ

SIHKLJS TAFPP TGHVO, FVO SAJ OJFO TAFPP DJ IFCTJO

CVWGIIHLSCDPJ, FVO RJ TAFPP DJ WAFVYJO.

1 WGICVSACFVT 15:51–52

Clue: S = T

Victory!

ABRMR MBEII KETR GEZ GFAB ABR IEKC, EOH ABR IEKC

MBEII LDRZSLKR ABRK: JLZ BR FM ILZH LJ ILZHM, EOH

TFOW LJ TFOWM: EOH ABRX ABEA EZR GFAB BFK EZR

SEIIRH, EOH SBLMRO, EOH JEFABJNI.

ZRDRIEAFLO 17:14   *Clue: T = K*

YUMLM YUNCVL N UBKM LQWDMC PCYW FWP, YUBY

NC TM FM TNVUY UBKM QMBOM. NC YUM RWIZH

FM LUBZZ UBKM YINAPZBYNWC: APY AM WS VWWH

OUMMI; N UBKM WKMIOWTM YUM RWIZH.

XWUC 16:33   *Clue: T = M*

165 The Patriarchs, Part 1

GSTCNSM ENYPP CND GYFS YGD FJMS LS QYPPSA

YLMYF, LKC CND GYFS ENYPP LS YLMYNYF; VJM Y

VYCNSM JV FYGD GYCTJGE NYBS T FYAS CNSS.

ISGSETE 17:5

Clue: G = N

C NR JES HUW UP NZYNENR JET PNJESY: PSNY LUJ,

PUY C NR GCJE JESS, NLW GCMM ZMSFF JESS, NLW

RAMJCKMT JET FSSW PUY RT FSYQNLJ NZYNENR'F

FNOS. NLW ES ZACMWSW NL NMJNY JESYS, NLW

BNMMSW AKUL JES LNRS UP JES MUYW, NLW

KCJBESW ECF JSLJ JESYS.

HSLSFCF 26:24–25

Clue: C = I

166 · The Patriarchs, Part 2

EUJVGX, K JOSU TUI IJU GOFX EURVAU DVM: YV KF

OFX HVTTUTT IJU GOFX PJKZJ IJU GVAX TPOAU MFIV

DVMA ROIJUAT, OEAOJOW, KTOOZ, OFX NOZVE, IV

YKSU MFIV IJUW OFX IV IJUKA TUUX ORIUA IJUW.

XUMIUAVFVWD 1:8   *Clue: E = B*

YHP EYDCL GCFSP Y GCF, OYBTHU, TV UCP FTII LS

FTKW RS, YHP FTII QSSA RS TH KWTO FYB KWYK T

UC, YHP FTII UTGS RS LNSYP KC SYK, YHP NYTRSHK KC

AMK CH, OC KWYK T DCRS YUYTH KC RB VYKWSN'O

WCMOS TH ASYDS; KWSH OWYII KWS ICNP LS RB UCP.

USHSOTO 28:20–21   *Clue: U = G*

167 Stormy Weather

FES, NMDXZS, JDMIM PFBM F WIMFJ HYES CIXB JDM

HYZSMIEMTT, FES TBXJM JDM CXRI PXIEMIT XC JDM

DXRTM, FES YJ CMZZ ROXE JDM GXREW BME, FES

JDMG FIM SMFS; FES Y XEZG FB MTPFOMS FZXEM JX

JMZZ JDMM.

VXN 1:19

Clue: J = T

WLVEJH, AVL JECH SODDLH WU, OKH O BCLOA OKH

DACEKB ZNKH CLKA AVL XEGKAONKD, OKH WCOML

NK SNLPLD AVL CEPMD WLQECL AVL JECH; WGA AVL

JECH ZOD KEA NK AVL ZNKH: OKH OQALC AVL ZNKH

OK LOCAVYGOML; WGA AVL JECH ZOD KEA NK AVL

LOCAVYGOML.

1 MNKBD 19:11

Clue: D = S

168 · *Raised from the Dead*

WMV QRVRF QMV VLRY ESS GJFVL, EHC AHRRSRC CJKH,

EHC QFEPRC; EHC VMFHZHU LZY VJ VLR WJCP IEZC,

VEWZVLE, EFZIR. EHC ILR JQRHRC LRF RPRI: EHC KLRH ILR

IEK QRVRF, ILR IEV MQ. EHC LR UEBR LRF LZI LEHC, EHC

SZGVRC LRF MQ, EHC KLRH LR LEC OESSRC VLR IEZHVI

EHC KZCJKI, QFRIRHVRC LRF ESZBR.

EOVI 9:40–41   *Clue: K = W*

FEG FI JFCN XFI NREQ JVPFSOHEQ, OP ICEZ GRXE

XHUO INPPJ, FEG KPNN GRXE KVRA UOP UOHVG

NRKU, FEG XFI UFZPE CJ GPFG. FEG JFCN XPEU GRXE,

FEG KPNN RE OHA, FEG PALVFSHEQ OHA IFHG,

UVRCLNP ERU BRCVIPNYPI; KRV OHI NHKP HI HE OHA.

FSUI 20:9–10   *Clue: J = P*

169 Taking an Offering

MJMHP XLR LNNBHTURA LI ZM VGHVBIMFZ UR ZUI

ZMLHF, IB OMF ZUX AUJM; RBF AHGTAURAOP, BH BC

RMNMIIUFP: CBH ABT OBJMFZ L NZMMHCGO AUJMH.

2 NBHURFZULRI 9:7

Clue: J = V

LPRAH BO JKK FIO FRFIOG RAFQ FIO GFQPOIQZGO,

FIJF FIOPO DJB LO DOJF RA DRAO IQZGO, JAV EPQWO

DO AQT IOPOTRFI, GJRFI FIO KQPV QM IQGFG, RM R

TRKK AQF QEOA BQZ FIO TRAVQTG QM IOJWOA, JAV

EQZP BQZ QZF J LKOGGRAH, FIJF FIOPO GIJKK AQF LO

PQQD OAQZHI FQ POUORWO RF.

DJKJUIR 3:10

Clue: D = M

170   *Quotable Ezra*

IBB VJGA IV AIL VTXIKIRTL RATQVTBMTV JFRS RATQ

HKSQ RAT HOBRAOFTVV SH RAT ATIRATF SH RAT BIFL,

RS VTTW RAT BSKL NSL SH OVKITB, LOL TIR, IFL WTXR

RAT HTIVR SH JFBTIMTFTL ZKTIL VTMTF LIDV PORA YSD.

TCKI 6:21–22   *Clue: G = C*

———————

GXB VYZN JR BKP LUTPOBO YZA CPHTBPO YZA IKTPR JR

BKP RYBKPUO, DKJ DPUP YZITPZB VPZ, BKYB KYA OPPZ

BKP RTUOB KJXOP, DKPZ BKP RJXZAYBTJZ JR BKTO KJXOP

DYO CYTA GPRJUP BKPTU PNPO, DPLB DTBK Y CJXA

HJTIP; YZA VYZN OKJXBPA YCJXA RJU SJN: OJ BKYB

BKP LPJLCP IJXCA ZJB ATOIPUZ BKP ZJTOP JR BKP OKJXB

JR SJN RUJV BKP ZJTOP JR BKP DPPLTZM JR BKP LPJLCP.

PEUY 3:12–13   *Clue: B = T*

171 *Troublemakers*

LFX MUBJB SLH FY SLMBJ WYJ MUB ZYFOJBOLMAYF: LFX

MUBE OLMUBJBX MUBNHBTKBH MYOBMUBJ LOLAFHM

NYHBH LFX LOLAFHM LLJYF. LFX MUB IBYITB ZUYXB

SAMU NYHBH, LFX HILPB, HLEAFO, SYGTX OYX MULM SB

ULX XABX SUBF YGJ RJBMUJBF XABX RBWYJB MUB TYJX!

FGNRBJH 20:2–3

Clue: O =G

———————

EKS OUI IEPOU RHIKIS UIP TRFOU, EKS QYEAARYIS OUIT

FH ORNIOUIP YMOU WRPEU, YUIK OUEO VRTHEKC

SMIS, YUEO OMTI OUI LMPI SIZRFPIS OYR UFKSPIS EKS

LMLOC TIK: EKS OUIC DIVETI E QMNK.

KFTDIPQ 26:10

Clue: Q = S

172) The Second Coming

SQI RUTQ BUSPP SMMTSV RUT BKFQ XC RUT BXQ XC

OSQ KQ UTSGTQ: SQI RUTQ BUSPP SPP RUT RVKATB XC

RUT TSVRU OXEVQ, SQI RUTW BUSPP BTT RUT BXQ XC

OSQ ZXOKQF KQ RUT ZPXEIB XC UTSGTQ LKRU MXLTV

SQI FVTSR FPXVW.

OSRRUTL 24:30   *Clue: O = M*

SZD HI DYKD VKW KCV DYKD YHZP TCHAUDY CH

FKC, CH, CHD DYU KCJUOL AYBRY KPU BC YUKEUC,

CUBDYUP DYU LHC, SZD DYU IKDYUP. DKTU WU YUUV,

AKDRY KCV QPKW: IHP WU TCHA CHD AYUC DYU

DBFU BL.

FKPT 13:32—33   *Clue: T = K*

173 A Common Woman's Name

ZA TWG GIZA GIL SMEQLTGLE'A AWT? ZA TWG IZA

NWGILE SMFFLB NMEO? MTB IZA CELGIELT, KMNLA,

MTB KWALA, MTB AZNWT, MTB KDBMA?

NMGGILR 13:55

Clue: E = R

_____

TCE MPUC GPU ITAATGP MTI XTIG, RTNH RTBETFUCU,

TCE RTNH GPU RKGPUN KL QTRUI, TCE ITFKRU, PTE

AKYBPG IMUUG IXDJUI, GPTG GPUH RDBPG JKRU TCE

TCKDCG PDR.

RTNO 16:1

Clue: R = M

174 God Provides

EGMFBHKT YPK WBWBKF PGC YPKD QTGC: YPKD

YGBW MGY, YPKD FXBM MGY; IMH DKY B FID SMYG

DGS, YPIY FGWGUGM BM IWW PBF QWGTD CIF MGY

ITTIDKH WBAK GMK GV YPKFK.

WSAK 12:27   *Clue: F = S*

V KSTG LGGA JICAF, SAO AIN SQ IUO; JGP KSTG V AIP

MGGA PKG WVFKPGICM BIWMSXGA, AIW KVM MGGO

LGFFVAF LWGSO.

DMSUQ 37:25   *Clue: W = R*

175 Important Questions

QLNB DL RTI, RLAIMLB HL NQBNAO: MNUL RTI A ITPO

IMLL QBTW IMNI IAWL, NRO MNUL OLJPNBLO AI? DL

NBL LULR WD YAIRLZZLZ. AZ IMLBL N STO HLZAOL WL?

DLN, IMLBL AZ RT STO; A XRTY RTI NRD.

AZNANM 44:8

Clue: D = Y

ZRS VUFO SUF DUNCYBFFB UNE UFNCE SUNS UF

UNE DRS SUF BNEERMFFB SW BYQFOMF, SUFH VFCF

XNSUFCFE SWXFSUFC. SUFO WOF WK SUFT, VUYMU

VNB N QNVHFC, NBPFE UYT N LRFBSYWO, SFTDSYOX

UYT, NOE BNHYOX, TNBSFC, VUYMU YB SUF XCFNS

MWTTNOETFOS YO SUF QNV?

TNSSUFV 22:34–36

Clue: V = W

Martyrs

EPW OLHQ IOSPHW IOHGLHP, MEYYAPB DGSP BSW, EPW

IEQAPB, YSTW NHIDI, THMHAFH XQ IGATAO. EPW LH

UPHHYHW WSRP, EPW MTAHW RAOL E YSDW FSAMH,

YSTW, YEQ PSO OLAI IAP OS OLHAT MLETBH. EPW RLHP

LH LEW IEAW OLAI, LH CHYY EIYHHG.

EMOI 7:59–60   *Clue: Y = L*

PDGT UGHG QPJWGF, PDGT UGHG QEUW EQNWFGH,

UGHG PGVZPGF, UGHG QBECW UCPD PDG QUJHF:

PDGT UEWFGHGF EYJNP CW QDGGZQSCWQ EWF

RJEPQSCWQ; YGCWR FGQPCPNPG, EMMBCLPGF,

PJHVGWPGF; (JM UDJV PDG UJHBF UEQ WJP UJHPDT).

DGYHGUQ 11:37–38   *Clue: E = A*

Bible Cryptograms

177 Dreamers

MAH WEMYMTE NMQH OAPT FTNDWE, Q EMGD

HYDMKDH M HYDMK, MAH PEDYD QN ATAD PEMP

UMA QAPDYWYDP QP: MAH Q EMGD EDMYH NMB TC

PEDD, PEMP PETO UMANP OAHDYNPMAH M HYDMK PT

QAPDYWYDP QP.

JDADNQN 41:15

Clue: W = P

TMU FA PSQU GP PS FGJ KTPFAB, TMU PS FGJ

CBAPFBAM: TMU FGJ KTPFAB BACWDAU FGV, TMU

JTGU WMPS FGV, NFTP GJ PFGJ UBATV PFTP PFSW

FTJP UBATVAU? JFTQQ G TMU PFR VSPFAB TMU PFR

CBAPFBAM GMUAAU LSVA PS CSN USNM SWBJAQZAJ

PS PFAA PS PFA ATBPF?

OAMAJGJ 37:10

Clue: C = B

178 A Word from Amos

UGS, VG, OL IORI UGSYLIO IOL YGDAIRBAJ, RAK

ZSLRILIO IOL FBAK, RAK KLZVRSLIO DAIG YRA FORI BJ

OBJ IOGDEOI, IORI YRPLIO IOL YGSABAE KRSPALJJ, RAK

ISLRKLIO DMGA IOL OBEO MVRZLJ GU IOL LRSIO, IOL

VGSK, IOL EGK GU OGJIJ, BJ OBJ ARYL.

RYGJ 4:13   *Clue: K = D*

OBTSTVMST OBT VKEWBO FBRKK YTSEFB VSMI OBT

FUEVO, RGC OBT FOSMGW FBRKK GMO FOSTGWOBTG

BEF VMSQT, GTEOBTS FBRKK OBT IEWBOA CTKEXTS

BEIFTKV: GTEOBTS FBRKK BT FORGC OBRO BRGCKTOB

OBT LMU; RGC BT OBRO EF FUEVO MV VMMO FBRKK

GMO CTKEXTS BEIFTKV: GTEOBTS FBRKK BT OBRO

SECTOB OBT BMSFT CTKEXTS BEIFTKV.

RIMF 2:14–15   *Clue: V = F*

179 The Opposite of Proud

FIDUBDSQDJFCBFY SKEKMBJS SHRPGKC SBRQKGT

TIZ DSK AZBCK IT SBQ SKJZD, PIDS SK JFC DSK

BFSJPBDJFDQ IT NKZHQJGKR, QI DSJD DSK UZJDS

IT DSK GIZC VJRK FID HAIF DSKR BF DSK CJWQ IT

SKEKMBJS.

2 VSZIFBVGKQ 32:26

Clue: G = L

SVDL RPS HERPIZ FCSV SVI FDPZH DW SVB GDLSV, SVDL

RPS SRAIE FCSV SVI FDPZH DW SVB GDLSV. ZD SVCH

EDF, GB HDE, REZ ZIKCTIP SVBHIKW, FVIE SVDL RPS

MDGI CESD SVI VREZ DW SVB WPCIEZ; XD, VLGNKI

SVBHIKW, REZ GRAI HLPI SVB WPCIEZ.

YPDTIPNH 6:2–3

Clue: L = U

Guilty!

KAT TS NKAT DOJD TOJD DOCKPR RASXSG DOS VJT

RJCDO, CD RJCDO DA DOSY TOA JGS IKMSG DOS VJT:

DOJD SXSGB YAIDO YJB ES RDAFFSM, JKM JVV DOS

TAGVM YJB ESLAYS PICVDB ESUAGS PAM.

GAYJKR 3:19   *Clue: V = L*

OKE FN JH GSZH LHMUHIE ER UHLMRTM, JH

IRBBFE MFT, STW SLH IRTZFTIHW RN EGH CSV SM

ELSTMQLHMMRLM. NRL VGRMRHZHL MGSCC AHHU EGH

VGRCH CSV, STW JHE RNNHTW FT RTH URFTE, GH FM

QKFCEJ RN SCC.

PSBHM 2:9–10   *Clue: R = O*

181 · *Forgiven!*

OSG LE AMF MFLQFH WE MWUM LPSQF AMF FLGAM,

ES UGFLA WE MWE CFGKR ASTLGY AMFC AMLA OFLG

MWC. LE OLG LE AMF FLEA WE OGSC AMF TFEA,

ES OLG MLAM MF GFCSQFY SBG AGLHEUGFEEWSHE

OGSC BE.

VELIC 103:11–12

Clue: A = T

GT CS YUL HAUH CS AUNS TSIIBCYAGF CGHA AGP,

UER CUIW GE RUOWESYY, CS IGS, UER RB EBH HAS

HOZHA: VZH GT CS CUIW GE HAS IGMAH, UY AS

GY GE HAS IGMAH, CS AUNS TSIIBCYAGF BES CGHA

UEBHASO, UER HAS VIBBR BT KSYZY DAOGYH AGY YBE

DISUEYSHA ZY TOBP UII YGE.

1 KBAE 1:6–7

Clue: S = E

182 *Gossip and Slander*

IJH M IDRH, TDGY, SCDB M AJXD, M GCRTT BJY IMBL

EJO GOAC RG M SJOTL, RBL YCRY M GCRTT UD IJOBL

OBYJ EJO GOAC RG ED SJOTL BJY: TDGY YCDHD UD

LDURYDG, DBNEMBPG, SHRYCG, GYHMIDG,

URAQUMYMBPG, SCMGZDHMBPG, GSDTTMBPG, YOXOTYG.

2 AJHMBYCMRBG 12:20   *Clue: I = F*

HIJB, PML AMNHH NKSBD SR CMI CNKDJRNOHD?

PML AMNHH BPDHH SR CMI MLHI MSHH? MD CMNC

PNHFDCM ETJSZMCHI, NRB PIJFDCM JSZMCDLEARDAA,

NRB ATDNFDCM CMD CJECM SR MSA MDNJC. MD

CMNC KNOFKSCDCM RLC PSCM MSA CLRZED, RIJ

BLDCM DWSH CL MSA RDSZMKLEJ.

TANHV 15:1–3   *Clue: P = W*

183 *What the World Needs Most*

AHC PA FDP DPQ LBZPO, XEL LA GAYC APC DPALBCT:

SAT BC LBDL GAYCLB DPALBCT BDLB SEGSZGGCR LBC

GDH.

TAFDPI 13:8

Clue: L = T

CNNSOY RN QEJN TABSHSNU RGAB CGADC SO

GKNRSOY MQN MBAMQ MQBGAYQ MQN CTSBSM

AOMG AOHNSYONU DGJN GH MQN KBNMQBNO,

CNN MQEM RN DGJN GON EOGMQNB ISMQ E TABN

QNEBM HNBJNOMDR: KNSOY KGBO EYESO, OGM GH

LGBBATMSKDN CNNU, KAM GH SOLGBBATMSKDN, KR

MQN IGBU GH YGU.

1 TNMNB 1:22–23

Clue: E = A

184) *Biblical Skyscrapers*

MW IOMGL LRKOILLU, PYMU EOMJ IOL IMELW RU

GRBMCJ HLBB, CUF GBLE IOLJ, IORUN DL IOCI IOLD

ELWL GRUULWG CAMZL CBB JLU IOCI FELBI RU

SLWPGCBLJ? R ILBB DMP, UCD: API, LTVLYI DL WLYLUI, DL

GOCBB CBB BRNLERGL YLWRGO.

BPNL 13:4–5   *Clue: D = Y*

RU CU, SNC HT POLN IAMDL, OGF IHAG CENP

CEUAUHRESB. OGF CENB EOF IAMDL WUA TCUGN,

OGF TSMPN EOF CENB WUA PUACNA. OGF CENB

TOMF, RU CU, SNC HT IHMSF HT O DMCB OGF O

CUXNA, XEUTN CUZ POB ANODE HGCU ENOJNG; OGF

SNC HT POLN HT O GOPN, SNTC XN IN TDOCCNANF

OIAUOF.

RNGNTMT 11:3–4   *Clue: F = D*

185 Advice from James

LSLU DK PEBNG, BP BN GENG UKN FKJOD, BD ALEA,

HLBUM ERKUL. TLE, E CEU CET DET, NGKI GEDN PEBNG,

EUA B GESL FKJOD: DGLF CL NGT PEBNG FBNGKIN

NGT FKJOD, EUA B FBRR DGLF NGLL CT PEBNG HT CT

FKJOD.

VECLD 2:17–18

Clue: C = M

_____

KILT VRGBDG DLTG VHIO HBC KFZRSFBZO HTLBZ ALN?

DLTG SRGA BLS RGBDG, GUGB LK ALNI MNOSO SRHS

VHI FB ALNI TGTEGIO? AG MNOS, HBC RHUG BLS: AG

PFMM, HBC CGOFIG SL RHUG, HBC DHBBLS LESHFB:

AG KFZRS HBC VHI, AGS AG RHUG BLS, EGDHNOG AG

HOP BLS.

QHTGO 4:1–2

Clue: D = C

186 *More Advice from James*

EJPUPGO NP VHLE HLF EJGF OJGQQ KP LH FJP SLUULE.

MLU EJGF AO NLYU QAMP? AF AO PWPH G WGBLYU,

FJGF GBBPGUPFJ MLU G QAFFQP FASP, GHI FJPH

WGHAOJPFJ GEGN. MLU FJGF NP LYCJF FL OGN, AM FJP

QLUI EAQQ, EP OJGQQ QAWP, GHI IL FJAO, LU FJGF.

TGSPO 4:14–15   *Clue: L = O*

IB LSNUBEN NJBVBOTVB, IVBNJVBE, KENT NJB YTRUEF

TO NJB ZTVH. IBJTZH, NJB JKPISEHRSE QSUNBNJ OTV

NJB LVBYUTKP OVKUN TO NJB BSVNJ, SEH JSNJ ZTEF

LSNUBEYB OTV UN, KENUZ JB VBYBUAB NJB BSVZC SEH

ZSNNBV VSUE. IB CB SZPT LSNUBEN; PNSIUZUPJ CTKV

JBSVNP: OTV NJB YTRUEF TO NJB ZTVH HVSQBNJ EUFJ.

MSRBP 5:7–8   *Clue: I = B*

187 Doubting Thomas

FPMD CTNFP PM FG FPGSTC, KMTLP PNFPMK FPB

HNDYMK, TDA WMPGJA SB PTDAC; TDA KMTLP PNFPMK

FPB PTDA, TDA FPKECF NF NDFG SB CNAM: TDA WM

DGF HTNFPJMCC, WEF WMJNMUNDY.

OGPD 20:27

Clue: C = S

MCFNF FHOUB NLUE BOS, UBESHF, ACIHNFC UBEN

BHFU FCCL SC, UBEN BHFU ACJOCDCK: AJCFFCK

HGC UBCT UBHU BHDC LEU FCCL, HLK TCU BHDC

ACJOCDCK.

MEBL 20:29

Clue: A = B

True Motivation

KUF IRKEDTCSCW NC FT AU ITWF TW FCCF, FT KHH AU

ERC UKGC TP ERC HTWF VCDLD, OASAUO ERKUYD ET

OTF KUF ERC PKERCW ZN RAG.

JTHTDDAKUD 3:17   *Clue: R = H*

DVA AECV, C PNK CT SCZ, TUBB AEBWB AEJKSW; NKZ

TCUUCO NTABL LJSEABCVWKBWW, SCZUJKBWW, TNJAE,

UCMB, GNAJBKFB, PBBIKBWW.

1 AJPCAEX 6:11   *Clue: S = G*

189 — A Biblical Queen

CPL NTHP UTH YMHHP KS FTHEC THCBL KS UTH SCDH

KS FKZKDKP GKPGHBPOPI UTH PCDH KS UTH ZKBL, FTH

GCDH UK JBKRH TOD NOUT TCBL YMHFUOKPF.

1 AOPIF 10:1

Clue: F = S

KAB OFBBL TR KAB UTFKA UAQCC GSUB FV SL KAB

NFZEPBLK DSKA KAB PBL TR KASU EBLBGQKSTL, QLZ

JTLZBPL KABP: RTG UAB JQPB RGTP KAB FKPTUK VQGKU

TR KAB BQGKA KT ABQG KAB DSUZTP TR UTCTPTL; QLZ,

YBATCZ, Q EGBQKBG KAQL UTCTPTL SU ABGB.

CFWB 11:31

Clue: G = R

Trees

RGO FUJN UJRLO FUJ ISCMJ SB FUJ ASLO HSO

DRAECGH CG FUJ HRLOJG CG FUJ MSSA SB FUJ ORN:

RGO RORV RGO UCP DCBJ UCO FUJVPJAIJP BLSV FUJ

YLJPJGMJ SB FUJ ASLO HSO RVSGHPF FUJ FLJJP SB FUJ

HRLOJG.

HJGJPCP 3:8   *Clue: A = L*

FAED RAMBF KEF UBMKF FASS M NOELS EH MKJ FOSSR

KSMO DKFE FAS MBFMO EH FAS BEOY FAJ NEY, CAPTA

FAED RAMBF ZMVS FASS.

YSDFSOEKEZJ 16:21   *Clue: D = U*

191

When Life Doesn't Make Sense

HAO YP BLASVLBI GOT FAB PASO BLASVLBI, FTUBLTO

GOT PASO KGPI YP KGPI, IGUBL BLT EAON. HAO GI BLT

LTGZTFI GOT LUVLTO BLGF BLT TGOBL, IA GOT YP KGPI

LUVLTO BLGF PASO KGPI, GFN YP BLASVLBI BLGF PASO

BLASVLBI.

UIGUGL 55:8–9   *Clue: T = E*

REAS UHT ISJKANAY REA DHNY, ISY JIGY, G VSHK REIR

REHM FISJR YH AOANB REGSC, ISY REIR SH REHMCER

FIS TA KGREEHDYAS PNHQ REAA. KEH GJ EA REIR

EGYARE FHMSJAD KGREHMR VSHKDAYCA? REANAPHNA

EIOA G MRRANAY REIR G MSYANJRHHY SHR; REGSCJ

RHH KHSYANPMD PHN QA, KEGFE G VSAK SHR.

UHT 42:1–3   *Clue: G = I*

192   *Rock and Roll*

OTCGC WABBSNT P KAN GTPMM EPMM NTSJSAH: PHW

TS NTPN JCMMSNT P GNCHS, AN OAMM JSNLJH LKCH

TAI.

KJCUSJXG 26:27   *Clue: C = O*

KAR, GNUBXR, SUNVN JKM K CVNKS NKVSUHOKTN:

PBV SUN KACNX BP SUN XBVR RNMENARNR PVBI

UNKWNA, KAR EKIN KAR VBXXNR GKET SUN MSBAN

PVBI SUN RBBV, KAR MKS ODBA FS.

IKSSUNJ 28:2   *Clue: R = D*

193 *What a Waste. . .*

KLBFOR AT KLBFOFUI, ILFOE OEU HCULMEUC, KLBFOR AT

KLBFOFUI; LPP FI KLBFOR. VELO HCATFO ELOE L JLB AT

LPP EFI PLDASC VEFME EU OLXUOE SBGUC OEU ISB?

UMMPUIFLIOUI 1:2–3   *Clue: A = O*

———————

NIA PORE HC R LRU WAINHEJG, HN OJ CORSS FRHU

EOJ POISJ PIASG, RUG SICJ OHC IPU CIQS? IA PORE

CORSS R LRU FHKJ HU JBMORUFJ NIA OHC CIQS?

LREEOJP 16:26   *Clue: F = G*

194 *Gimme a Sign*

TCB GWDFLC VPFGGFB NOFD, TCB GTWB MCNL DTJE

OWG DLNOFJ, VFOLPB, NOWG IOWPB WG GFN KLJ

NOF KTPP TCB JWGWCS TSTWC LK DTCE WC WGJTFP;

TCB KLJ T GWSC AOWIO GOTPP VF GRLHFC TSTWCGN.

PMHF 2:34   *Clue: J = R*

———————

LRF MB ICTVBABN ICN TISN RCFD FMBH, IC BXSE ICN

INREFBADRT JBCBAIFSDC TBBPBFM IGFBA I TSJC; ICN

FMBAB TMIEE CD TSJC LB JSXBC FD SF, LRF FMB TSJC

DG FMB KADKMBF UDCIT.

HIFFMBV 12:39   *Clue: L = B*

Bible Study

LABPDT ITA LDPNRIGPAL; CEP NO ITAH MA ITNOX

MA TBSA AIAPOBJ JNCA: BOU ITAM BPA ITAM YTNDT

IALINCM EC HA.

VETO 5:39   *Clue: T = H*

BRH DLJ NMJDLMJR CUUJHCBDJEA FJRD BQBA SBPE BRH

FCEBF NA RCKLD PRDI NJMJB: QLI TIUCRK DLCDLJM

QJRD CRDI DLJ FARBKIKPJ IO DLJ GJQF. DLJFJ QJMJ

UIMJ RINEJ DLBR DLIFJ CR DLJFFBEIRCTB, CR DLBD DLJA

MJTJCXJH DLJ QIMH QCDL BEE MJBHCRJFF IO UCRH,

BRH FJBMTLJH DLJ FTMCSDPMJF HBCEA.

BTDF 17:10–11   *Clue: H = D*

196 *God's Weatlh*

BEA PRSJAH RP LRFA, UFK BEA CGSK RP LRFA, PURBE

BEA SGHK GD EGPBP.

EUCCUR 2:8   *Clue: P = S*

GDN AJANO MAHBP DG PIA GDNABP UB XURA,

HRC PIA THPPQA EZDR H PIDEBHRC IUQQB. U LRDS

HQQ PIA GDSQB DG PIA XDERPHURB: HRC PIA SUQC

MAHBPB DG PIA GUAQC HNA XURA. UG U SANA

IERVNO, U SDEQC RDP PAQQ PIAA: GDN PIA SDNQC

UB XURA, HRC PIA GEQRABB PIANADG.

ZBHQX 50:10–12   *Clue: X = M*

197 — *Dirty Birds*

IOM NCPGP IAP NCPL ECTZC LP GCIBB CISP TO

IVFHTOINTFO IHFOK NCP UFEBG; NCPL GCIBB OFN VP

PINPO, NCPL IAP IO IVFHTOINTFO: NCP PIKBP, IOM NCP

FGGTUAIKP, IOM NCP FGDAIL.

BPSTNTZYG 11:13

Clue: V = B

Y FYEE DYKC MRCC VPMS MRC IHKCPSVO LYIGO SJ

CKCIQ OSIM, HPG MS MRC LCHOMO SJ MRC JYCEG

MS LC GCKSVICG.

CXCUYCE 39:4

Clue: L = B

Nice Birds

LAW FSM MOS DULAASOD DSRN YSA L YLAMVEFB?

LFN SFW SY MVWC DVLRR FSM YLRR SF MVW BASPFN

OEMVSPM HSPA YLMVWA.

CLMMVWO 10:29

Clue: U = P

UCF AHSRFEK DLLFDE ST UCF FDEUC; UCF UPBF SA UCF

KPTXPTX SA JPEYK PK OSBF, DTY UCF MSPOF SA UCF

UWEUHF PK CFDEY PT SWE HDTY.

KSTX SA KSHSBST 2:12

Clue: H = L

199 Important Terms

KRL SU MO PSU IHTIMPMKPMTR ATH TGH OMRO: KRL

RTP ATH TGHO TRBF, EGP KBOT ATH PSU OMRO TA PSU

JSTBU JTHBL.

1 NTSR 2:2

Clue: M = I

CXE CLA POWQSOHOP GEH EJH EGGOIBOA, LIP CLA

HLQAOP LFLQI GEH EJH RJAKQGQBLKQEI.

HEDLIA 4:25

Clue: I = N

Handwritten annotation: WHO WAS DELIVERED FOR OUR OFFENCES AND WAS RAISED AGAIN FOR OUR JUSTIFICATION. ROMANS

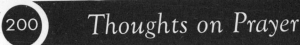

Thoughts on Prayer

UC PHDAR NTLEO OTHM TRLI DK OTR UHIKDKB, H EHIF;

DK OTR UHIKDKB GDEE D FDIRAO UC SILCRI MKOH

OTRR, LKF GDEE EHHX MS.

SNLEU 5:3   *Clue: C = Y*

LBR CSPJEWEPR TW LBR AEPQRF EC SO SNTHEOSLETO

LT LBR DTJF: NIL LBR GJSXRJ TW LBR IGJEKBL EC BEC

FRDEKBL.

GJTMRJNC 15:8   *Clue: F = D*

201 Jesus' Power

CGG FMJOIH QYAY RAYCFYU SB MJP, COU TEA MJP:

COU MY JH SYTEAY CGG FMJOIH, COU SB MJP CGG

FMJOIH REOHJHF.

REGEHHJCOH 1:16–17

Clue: E = O

_____

PEGP GP PEN DGON LK BNIAI NUNHR QDNN IELASV

FLC, LK PEMDJI MD ENGUND, GDV PEMDJI MD NGHPE,

GDV PEMDJI ADVNH PEN NGHPE.

TEMSMTTMGDI 2:10

Clue: L = O

202 *Saving the Best for Last*

GASU OTWBU DSGSY JUOHSYSI ATW, FBYI, GB HABW

OAJFF HS EB? GABM AJOG GAS HBYIO BV SGSYUJF

FTVS.

KBAU 6:68   *Clue: II = W*

JSCY QFHJ RSAQ UA JSA BNJS CP HFPA: FM JST

BDARAMIA FR PYHMARR CP OCT; NJ JST DFLSJ SNME

JSADA NDA BHANRYDAR PCD AKADUCDA.

BRNHU 16:11   *Clue: F = I*

Bible Cryptogram Answer Key

1) Born Again!

For I am not ashamed of the gospel of Christ: for it is the power of God unto salvation to every one that believeth; to the Jew first, and also to the Greek. ROMANS 1:16

But we are bound to give thanks alway to God for you, brethren beloved of the Lord, because God hath from the beginning chosen you to salvation through sanctification of the Spirit and belief of the truth. 2 THESSALONIANS 2:13

2) The Key Ingredient

And Jesus said unto him, Go thy way; thy faith hath made thee whole. And immediately he received his sight, and followed Jesus in the way. MARK 10:52

For therein is the righteousness of God revealed from faith to faith: as it is written, The just shall live by faith. ROMANS 1:17

3) A Wing and a Prayer

Our soul is escaped as a bird out of the snare of the fowlers: the snare is broken, and we are escaped. PSALM 124:7

Curse not the king, no not in thy thought; and curse not the rich in thy bedchamber: for a bird of the air shall carry the voice, and that which hath wings shall tell the matter. ECCLESIASTES 10:20

4) A Very Important Person

And the child grew, and she brought him unto Pharaoh's daughter, and he became her son. And she called his name Moses: and she said, Because I drew him out of the water. EXODUS 2:10

By faith Moses, when he was come to years, refused to be called the son of Pharaoh's daughter; choosing rather to suffer affliction with the people of God, than to enjoy the pleasures of sin for a season. HEBREWS 11:24–25

5) Keep Looking Up

Behold, the eye of the LORD is upon them that fear him, upon them that hope in his mercy. PSALM 33:18

Blessed be the God and Father of our Lord Jesus Christ, which according to his abundant mercy hath begotten us again unto a lively hope by the resurrection of Jesus Christ from the dead. 1 PETER 1:3

6) Lives Changed

Now when they saw the boldness of Peter and John, and perceived that they were unlearned and ignorant men, they marvelled; and they took knowledge of them, that they had been with Jesus. ACTS 4:13

And Zacchaeus stood, and said unto the Lord; Behold, Lord, the half of my goods I give to the poor; and if I have taken any thing from any man by false accusation, I restore him fourfold. And Jesus said unto him, This day is salvation come to this house. LUKE 19:8–9

7) Powerful Stuff

My soul cleaveth unto the dust: quicken thou me according to thy word. PSALM 119:25

For the word of God is quick, and powerful, and sharper than any twoedged sword, piercing even to the dividing asunder of soul and spirit, and of the joints and marrow, and is a discerner of the thoughts and intents of the heart. HEBREWS 4:12

8) Good Kings

And thus did Hezekiah throughout all Judah, and wrought that which was good and right and truth before the LORD his God. 2 CHRONICLES 31:20

And Josiah took away all the abominations out of all the countries that pertained to the children of Israel, and made all that were present in Israel to serve, even to serve the LORD their God. 2 CHRONICLES 34:33

9) Bad Kings

But he did that which was evil in the sight of the LORD, as did Manasseh his father: for Amon sacrificed unto all the carved images which Manasseh his father had made, and served them. 2 CHRONICLES 33:22

And Ahab the son of Omri did evil in the sight of the LORD above all that were before him. 1 KINGS 16:30

10) Spiritual Fruit

Even so every good tree bringeth forth good fruit; but a corrupt tree bringeth forth evil fruit. MATTHEW 7:17

But now being made free from sin, and become servants to God, ye have your fruit unto holiness, and the end everlasting life. ROMANS 6:22

11) Simon Says

And Simon Peter answered and said, Thou art the Christ, the Son of the living God. MATTHEW 16:16

Peter said unto him, Lord, why cannot I follow thee now? I will lay down my life for thy sake. JOHN 13:37

12) The Flood

And God said unto Noah, The end of all flesh is come before me; for the earth is filled with violence through them; and, behold, I will destroy them with the earth. GENESIS 6:13

And Noah did according unto all that the LORD commanded him. GENESIS 7:5

13) Old Testament Miracles

And the LORD said unto Moses, Stretch out thine hand toward heaven, that there may be darkness over the land of Egypt, even darkness which may be felt. EXODUS 10:21

And it came to pass, as they were burying a man, that, behold, they spied a band of men; and they cast the man into the sepulchre of Elisha: And when the man was let down, and touched the bones of Elisha, he revived, and stood up on his feet. 2 KINGS 13:21

14) The End of Time

And many of them that sleep in the dust of the earth shall awake, some to everlasting life, and some to shame and everlasting contempt. DANIEL 12:2

And I saw a new heaven and a new earth: for the first heaven and the first earth were passed away; and there was no more sea. REVELATION 21:1

15) Great Stuff from the Psalms

For the LORD knoweth the way of the righteous: but the way of the ungodly shall perish. PSALM 1:6

It is a good thing to give thanks unto the LORD, and to sing praises unto thy name, O most High: To shew forth thy lovingkindness in the morning, and thy faithfulness every night. PSALM 92:1–2

16) More Great Stuff from the Psalms

There is a river, the streams whereof shall make glad the city of God, the holy place of the tabernacles of the most High. PSALM 46:4

Praise ye the LORD. Praise God in his sanctuary: praise him in the firmament of his power. Praise him for his mighty acts: praise him according to his excellent greatness. PSALM 150:1–2

17) John the Baptist

For I say unto you, Among those that are born of women there is not a greater prophet than John the Baptist: but he that is least in the kingdom of God is greater than he. LUKE 7:28

For John the Baptist came neither eating bread nor drinking wine; and ye say, He hath a devil. The Son of man is come eating and drinking; and ye say, Behold a gluttonous man, and a winebibber, a friend of publicans and sinners! LUKE 7:33–34

18) Precious Metals

Ye shall not make with me gods of silver, neither shall ye make unto you gods of gold. EXODUS 20:23

And the twelve gates were twelve pearls: every several gate was of one pearl: and the street of the city was pure gold, as it were transparent glass. REVELATION 21:21

19) Hey, Good Lookin'

But in all Israel there was none to be so much praised as Absalom for his beauty: from the sole of his foot even to the crown of his head there was no blemish in him. 2 SAMUEL 14:25

And he brought up Hadassah, that is, Esther, his uncle's daughter: for she had neither father nor mother, and the maid was fair and beautiful; whom Mordecai, when her father and mother were dead, took for his own daughter. ESTHER 2:7

20) Prophets in General

And he said, Hear now my words: If there be a prophet among you, I the LORD will make myself known unto him in a vision, and will speak unto him in a dream. NUMBERS 12: 6

But the prophet, which shall presume to speak a word in my name, which I have not commanded him to speak, or that shall speak in the name of other gods, even that prophet shall die. DEUTERONOMY 18:20

21) Prophets in Specific

And they told the king, saying, Behold Nathan the prophet. And when he was come in before the king, he bowed himself before the king with his face to the ground. 1 KINGS 1:23

How long halt ye between two opinions? if the LORD be God, follow him: but if Baal, then follow him. And the people answered him not a word. Then said Elijah unto the people, I, even I only, remain a prophet of the LORD; but Baal's prophets are four hundred and fifty men. 1 KINGS 18:21–22

22) More Prophets in Specific

In those days was Hezekiah sick unto death. And Isaiah the prophet the son of Amoz came unto him, and said unto him, Thus saith the LORD, Set thine house in order: for thou shalt die, and not live. ISAIAH 38:1

Even the prophet Jeremiah said, Amen: the LORD do so: the LORD perform thy words which thou hast prophesied, to bring again the vessels of the LORD's house, and all that is carried away captive, from Babylon into this place. JEREMIAH 28:6

23) Key Ideas of the New Testament

Now there are diversities of gifts, but the same Spirit. And there are differences of

administrations, but the same Lord. And there are diversities of operations, but it is the same God which worketh all in all.
1 CORINTHIANS 12:4–6

And every priest standeth daily ministering and offering oftentimes the same sacrifices, which can never take away sins: But this man, after he had offered one sacrifice for sins for ever, sat down on the right hand of God.
HEBREWS 10:11–12

24) Cleanliness Is Next to Godliness

He shall therefore burn that garment, whether warp or woof, in woollen or in linen, or any thing of skin, wherein the plague is: for it is a fretting leprosy; it shall be burnt in the fire.
LEVITICUS 13:52

And the leper in whom the plague is, his clothes shall be rent, and his head bare, and he shall put a covering upon his upper lip, and shall cry, Unclean, unclean. All the days wherein the plague shall be in him he shall be defiled; he is unclean: he shall dwell alone.
LEVITICUS 13:45–46

25) Verses Worth Memorizing

But God commendeth his love toward us, in that, while we were yet sinners, Christ died for us.
ROMANS 5:8

Be not deceived; God is not mocked: for whatsoever a man soweth, that shall he also reap. For he that soweth to his flesh shall of the flesh reap corruption; but he that soweth to the Spirit shall of the Spirit reap life everlasting.
GALATIANS 6:7–8

26) Attributes of God

Now unto the King eternal, immortal, invisible, the only wise God, be honour and glory for ever and ever. Amen. 1 TIMOTHY 1:17

Then came the word of the LORD unto Jeremiah, saying, Behold, I am the LORD, the God of all flesh: is there any thing too hard for me?
JEREMIAH 32:26–27

27) Real Smarts

The fear of the LORD is the beginning of wisdom: a good understanding have all they that do his commandments: his praise endureth for ever. PSALM 111:10

Wisdom is the principal thing; therefore get wisdom: and with all thy getting get understanding.
PROVERBS 4:7

28) Jonah's Story

Arise, go to Nineveh, that great city, and cry against it; for their wickedness is come up before me. But Jonah rose up to flee unto Tarshish from the presence of the LORD, and went down to Joppa. Jonah 1:2–3

I cried by reason of mine affliction unto the LORD, and he heard me; out of the belly of hell cried I, and thou heardest my voice. For thou hadst cast me into the deep, in the midst of the seas; and the floods compassed me about. JONAH 2:2–3

29) Lamentable

How hath the LORD covered the daughter of Zion with a cloud in his anger, and cast down from heaven unto the earth the beauty of Israel, and remembered not his footstool in the day of his anger!
LAMENTATIONS 2:1

For the LORD will not cast off for ever: But though he cause grief, yet will he have compassion according to the multitude of his mercies. LAMENTATIONS 3:31–32

30) Parables of Jesus

And he spake a parable unto them, Can the blind lead the blind? shall they not both fall into the ditch? LUKE 6:39

The kingdom of heaven is like to a grain of mustard seed, which a man took, and sowed in his field: Which

indeed is the least of all seeds: But when it is grown, it is the greatest among herbs, and becometh a tree, so that the birds of the air come and lodge in the branches thereof.
MATTHEW 13:31–32

31) More Parables of Jesus

Another parable spake he unto them; The kingdom of heaven is like unto leaven, which a woman took, and hid in three measures of meal, till the whole was leavened.
MATTHEW 13:33

Now learn a parable of the fig tree; when his branch is yet tender, and putteth forth leaves, ye know that summer is nigh: So likewise ye, when ye shall see all these things, know that it is near, even at the doors. MATTHEW 24:32–33

32) Jewelry in the Bible

And they came, both men and women, as many as were willing hearted, and brought bracelets, and earrings, and rings, and tablets, all jewels of gold: and every man that offered offered an offering of gold unto the LORD.
EXODUS 35:22

In that day the Lord will take away the bravery of their tinkling ornaments about their feet. . .the chains, and the bracelets, and the mufflers, the bonnets, and the ornaments of the legs, and the headbands, and the tablets, and the earrings, the rings, and nose jewels. ISAIAH 3:18–21

33) Old Folks

And Lamech lived after he begat Noah five hundred ninety and five years, and begat sons and daughters: And all the days of Lamech were seven hundred seventy and seven years: and he died. GENESIS 5:30–31

And Methuselah lived an hundred eighty and seven years, and begat Lamech. And Methuselah lived after he begat Lamech seven hundred eighty and two years, and begat sons and daughters: And all the days of Methuselah were nine hundred sixty and nine years: and he died. GENESIS 5:25–27

34) Theology of Romans, Part 1

Therefore by the deeds of the law there shall no flesh be justified in his sight: for by the law is the knowledge of sin. ROMANS 3:20

For the invisible things of him from the creation of the world are clearly seen, being understood by the things that are made, even his eternal power and Godhead; so that they are without excuse: Because that, when they knew God, they glorified him not as God, neither were thankful; but became vain in their imaginations. ROMANS 1:20–21

35) Theology of Romans, Part 2

For if, when we were enemies, we were reconciled to God by the death of his Son, much more, being reconciled, we shall be saved by his life. ROMANS 5:10

There is therefore now no condemnation to them which are in Christ Jesus, who walk not after the flesh, but after the Spirit. For the law of the Spirit of life in Christ Jesus hath made me free from the law of sin and death. ROMANS 8:1–2

36) Marital Mismatch

Now the name of the man was Nabal; and the name of his wife Abigail: and she was a woman of good understanding, and of a beautiful countenance: But the man was churlish and evil in his doings; and he was of the house of Caleb. 1 SAMUEL 25:3

Then his father and his mother said unto him, Is there never a woman among the daughters of thy brethren, or among all my people, that thou goest to take a wife of the uncircumcised Philistines? And Samson said unto his father, Get her for me; for she pleaseth me well. JUDGES 14:3

37) Gospel Villain

Then entered Satan into Judas surnamed Iscariot, being of the number of the twelve. And he went his way, and communed with the chief priests and captains, how he might betray him unto them. LUKE 22:3–4

Saying, I have sinned in that I have betrayed the innocent blood. And they said, What is that to us? see thou to that. And he cast down the pieces of silver in the temple, and departed, and went and hanged himself. MATTHEW 27:4–5

38) Thoughts for Philemon

I Paul have written it with mine own hand, I will repay it: albeit I do not say to thee how thou owest unto me even thine own self besides. PHILEMON 1:19

I thank my God, making mention of thee always in my prayers, hearing of thy love and faith, which thou hast toward the Lord Jesus, and toward all saints; that the communication of thy faith may become effectual by the acknowledging of every good thing which is in you in Christ Jesus. PHILEMON 1:4–6

39) Goats in the Bible

Or if his sin, which he hath sinned, come to his knowledge: Then he shall bring his offering, a kid of the goats, a female without blemish, for his sin which he hath sinned. LEVITICUS 4:28

Then Saul took three thousand chosen men out of all Israel, and went to seek David and his men upon the rocks of the wild goats. 1 SAMUEL 24:2

40) Days of Creation

And God said, Let there be lights in the firmament of the heaven to divide the day from the night; and let them be for signs, and for seasons, and for days, and years: And let them be for lights in the firmament of the heaven to give light upon the earth: and it was so. GENESIS 1:14–15

And God created great whales, and every living creature that moveth, which the waters brought forth abundantly, after their kind, and every winged fowl after his kind: and God saw that it was good. And God blessed them, saying, Be fruitful, and multiply. GENESIS 1:21–22

41) Cities in Acts

And a certain woman named Lydia, a seller of purple, of the city of Thyatira, which worshipped God, heard us: whose heart the Lord opened, that she attended unto the things which were spoken of Paul. ACTS 16:14

And the brethren immediately sent away Paul and Silas by night unto Berea: who coming thither went into the synagogue of the Jews. ACTS 17:10

42) Old Testament Mothers

Wherefore it came to pass, when the time was come about after Hannah had conceived, that she bare a son, and called his name Samuel, saying, Because I have asked him of the LORD. 1 SAMUEL 1:20

And Hagar bare Abram a son: and Abram called his son's name, which Hagar bare, Ishmael. GENESIS 16:15

43) More Old Testament Mothers

For Sarah conceived, and bare Abraham a son in his old age, at the set time of which God had spoken to him. GENESIS 21:2

So Boaz took Ruth, and she was his wife: and when he went in unto her, the LORD gave her conception, and she bare a son. RUTH 4:13

44) Jesus' Words to the Churches

So then because thou art lukewarm, and neither cold nor

hot, I will spue thee out of my mouth. Revelation 3:16

He that overcometh, the same shall be clothed in white raiment; and I will not blot out his name out of the book of life, but I will confess his name before my Father, and before his angels. Revelation 3:5

45) Animals of the Bible

Every three years once came the ships of Tarshish bringing gold, and silver, ivory, and apes, and peacocks. 2 Chronicles 9:21

The wolf also shall dwell with the lamb, and the leopard shall lie down with the kid; and the calf and the young lion and the fatling together; and a little child shall lead them. Isaiah 11:6

46) Miracles of Paul

And God wrought special miracles by the hands of Paul: So that from his body were brought unto the sick handkerchiefs or aprons, and the diseases departed from them, and the evil spirits went out of them. Acts 19:11–12

And it came to pass, that the father of Publius lay sick of a fever and of a bloody flux: to whom Paul entered in, and prayed, and laid his hands on him, and healed him. Acts 28:8

47) Proverbially Speaking, Part 1

When wisdom entereth into thine heart, and knowledge is pleasant unto thy soul; discretion shall preserve thee, understanding shall keep thee. Proverbs 2:10–11

The blessing of the Lord, it maketh rich, and he addeth no sorrow with it. Proverbs 10:22

48) Proverbially Speaking, Part 2

How much better is it to get wisdom than gold! and to get understanding rather to be chosen than silver! Proverbs 16:16

Make no friendship with an angry man; and with a furious man thou shalt not go: Lest thou learn his ways, and get a snare to thy soul. Proverbs 22:24–25

49) Ex-Queens

And the king loved Esther above all the women, and she obtained grace and favour in his sight more than all the virgins; so that he set the royal crown upon her head, and made her queen instead of Vashti. Esther 2:17

Wherefore they came again, and told him. And he said, This is the word of the Lord, which he spake by his servant Elijah the Tishbite, saying, In the portion of Jezreel shall dogs eat the flesh of Jezebel. 2 Kings 9:36

50) A Note from Jude

Beloved, when I gave all diligence to write unto you of the common salvation, it was needful for me to write unto you, and exhort you that ye should earnestly contend for the faith which was once delivered unto the saints. Jude 1:3

Now unto him that is able to keep you from falling, and to present you faultless before the presence of his glory with exceeding joy, to the only wise God our Saviour, be glory and majesty, dominion and power. Jude 1:24–25

51) Ezekiel's Visions

The hand of the Lord was upon me, and carried me out in the spirit of the Lord, and set me down in the midst of the valley which was full of bones. Ezekiel 37:1

And I looked, and, behold, a whirlwind came out of the north, a great cloud, and a fire infolding itself, and a brightness was about it, and out of the midst thereof as the colour of amber, out of the midst of the fire. Also out of the midst thereof came the likeness of four living creatures. And this was their appearance; they had the likeness of a man. Ezekiel 1:4–5

52) On the Menu

And when the children of Israel saw it, they said one to another, It is manna: for they wist not what it was. And Moses said unto them, This is the bread which the Lord hath given you to eat. Exodus 16:15

And John was clothed with camel's hair, and with a girdle of a skin about his loins; and he did eat locusts and wild honey. Mark 1:6

53) Off the Menu

Ye shall not eat of any thing that dieth of itself: thou shalt give it unto the stranger that is in thy gates, that he may eat it. Deuteronomy 14:21

And the swine, though he divide the hoof, and be clovenfooted, yet he cheweth not the cud; he is unclean to you. Leviticus 11:7

54) Modes of Transportation

Tell ye the daughter of Sion, Behold, thy King cometh unto thee, meek, and sitting upon an ass, and a colt the foal of an ass. Matthew 21:5

And Joseph made ready his chariot, and went up to meet Israel his father, to Goshen, and presented himself unto him; and he fell on his neck, and wept on his neck a good while. Genesis 46:29

55) 2 Corinthians

While we look not at the things which are seen, but at the things which are not seen: for the things which are seen are temporal; but the things which are not seen are eternal.
2 Corinthians 4:18

Examine yourselves, whether ye be in the faith; prove your own selves. Know ye not your own selves, how that Jesus Christ is in you, except ye be reprobates? 2 Corinthians 13:5

56) The Number of Perfection

And God blessed the seventh day,

and sanctified it: because that in it he had rested from all his work which God created and made. GENESIS 2:3

And there came unto me one of the seven angels which had the seven vials full of the seven last plagues, and talked with me, saying, Come hither, I will shew thee the bride, the Lamb's wife. REVELATION 21:9

57) Poor Job, Part 1

And the LORD said unto Satan, Hast thou considered my servant Job, that there is none like him in the earth, a perfect and an upright man, one that feareth God, and escheweth evil? JOB 1:8

Then Satan answered the LORD, and said, Doth Job fear God for nought? Hast not thou made an hedge about him, and about his house, and about all that he hath on every side? JOB 1:9–10

58) Poor Job, Part 2

So they sat down with him upon the ground seven days and seven nights, and none spake a word unto him: for they saw that his grief was very great. JOB 2:13

Then Job arose, and rent his mantle, and shaved his head, and fell down upon the ground, and worshipped, and said, Naked came I out of my mother's womb, and naked shall I return thither: The LORD gave, and the LORD hath taken away. JOB 1:20–21

59) Job Restored

Then Job answered the LORD, and said, I know that thou canst do every thing, and that no thought can be withholden from thee. JOB 42:1–2

So the LORD blessed the latter end of Job more than his beginning: for he had fourteen thousand sheep, and six thousand camels, and a thousand yoke of oxen, and a thousand she asses. He had also seven sons and three daughters. JOB 42:12–13

60) The Crucifixion

And when they were come to the place, which is called Calvary, there they crucified him, and the malefactors, one on the right hand, and the other on the left. LUKE 23:33

And after that they had mocked him, they took the robe off from him, and put his own raiment on him, and led him away to crucify him. And as they came out, they found a man of Cyrene, Simon by name: Him they compelled to bear his cross. MATTHEW 27:31–32

61) Gideon

Behold, I will put a fleece of wool in the floor; and if the dew be on the fleece only, and it be dry upon all the earth beside, then shall I know that thou wilt save Israel by mine hand, as thou hast said. JUDGES 6:37

And the three companies blew the trumpets, and brake the pitchers, and held the lamps in their left hands, and the trumpets in their right hands to blow withal: And they cried, The sword of the LORD, and of Gideon. JUDGES 7:20

62) Temptation

There hath no temptation taken you but such as is common to man: But God is faithful, who will not suffer you to be tempted above that ye are able; but will with the temptation also make a way to escape, that ye may be able to bear it. 1 CORINTHIANS 10:13

Be sober, be vigilant; because your adversary the devil, as a roaring lion, walketh about, seeking whom he may devour: whom resist stedfast in the faith. 1 PETER 5:8–9

63) Framed!

And Ahab came into his house heavy and displeased because of the word which Naboth the Jezreelite had spoken to him: for he had said, I will not give thee the inheritance of my fathers. . . . But

Jezebel his wife came to him, and said unto him, Why is thy spirit so sad, that thou eatest no bread? 1 KINGS 21:4–5

Proclaim a fast, and set Naboth on high among the people: And set two men, sons of Belial, before him, to bear witness against him, saying, Thou didst blaspheme God and the king. And then carry him out, and stone him. 1 KINGS 21:9–10

64) Protecting Marriage

Drink waters out of thine own cistern, and running waters out of thine own well. PROVERBS 5:15

Let thy fountain be blessed: and rejoice with the wife of thy youth. Let her be as the loving hind and pleasant roe; let her breasts satisfy thee at all times; and be thou ravished always with her love. PROVERBS 5:18–19

65) From the Book of Galatians

Christ hath redeemed us from the curse of the law, being made a curse for us: for it is written, Cursed is every one that hangeth on a tree. GALATIANS 3:13

Knowing that a man is not justified by the works of the law, but by the faith of Jesus Christ, even we have believed in Jesus Christ, that we might be justified by the faith of Christ, and not by the works of the law: for by the works of the law shall no flesh be justified. GALATIANS 2:16

66) Snakes in the Bible

Therefore the people came to Moses, and said, We have sinned, for we have spoken against the LORD, and against thee; pray unto the LORD, that he take away the serpents from us. And Moses prayed for the people. NUMBERS 21:7

And when Paul had gathered a bundle of sticks, and laid them on the fire, there came a viper out of the heat, and fastened on his hand. ACTS 28:3

67) True Beauty

Who can find a virtuous woman? for her price is far above rubies. The heart of her husband doth safely trust in her, so that he shall have no need of spoil. PROVERBS 31:10–11

Whose adorning let it not be that outward adorning of plaiting the hair, and of wearing of gold, or of putting on of apparel; but let it be the hidden man of the heart, in that which is not corruptible, even the ornament of a meek and quiet spirit. 1 PETER 3:3–4

68) A Little R & R

The sleep of a labouring man is sweet, whether he eat little or much: but the abundance of the rich will not suffer him to sleep. ECCLESIASTES 5:12

And he said unto them, Come ye yourselves apart into a desert place, and rest a while: for there were many coming and going, and they had no leisure so much as to eat. MARK 6:31

69) Quotable Exodus

I am the LORD thy God, which have brought thee out of the land of Egypt, out of the house of bondage. Thou shalt have no other gods before me. EXODUS 20:2–3

And he said, I will make all my goodness pass before thee, and I will proclaim the name of the LORD before thee; and will be gracious to whom I will be gracious, and will shew mercy on whom I will shew mercy. EXODUS 33:19

70) Friends of Jesus

Now Jesus loved Martha, and her sister, and Lazarus. When he had heard therefore that he was sick, he abode two days still in the same place where he was. JOHN 11:5–6

One of the two which heard John speak, and followed him, was Andrew, Simon Peter's brother. He first findeth his own brother Simon, and saith unto him, We have found the Messias, which is, being interpreted, the Christ. JOHN 1:40–41

71) Animal Miracles

And the LORD opened the mouth of the ass, and she said unto Balaam, What have I done unto thee, that thou hast smitten me these three times? NUMBERS 22:28

Notwithstanding, lest we should offend them, go thou to the sea, and cast an hook, and take up the fish that first cometh up; and when thou hast opened his mouth, thou shalt find a piece of money: that take, and give unto them for me and thee. MATTHEW 17:27

72) Secretaries

Then Jeremiah called Baruch the son of Neriah: and Baruch wrote from the mouth of Jeremiah all the words of the LORD, which he had spoken unto him, upon a roll of a book. JEREMIAH 36:4

I Tertius, who wrote this epistle, salute you in the Lord. ROMANS 16:22

73) The Night Sky

Which maketh Arcturus, Orion, and Pleiades, and the chambers of the south. Which doeth great things past finding out; yea, and wonders without number. JOB 9:9–10

Therefore sprang there even of one, and him as good as dead, so many as the stars of the sky in multitude, and as the sand which is by the sea shore innumerable. HEBREWS 11:12

74) First Christmas

Now all this was done, that it might be fulfilled which was spoken of the Lord by the prophet, saying, Behold, a virgin shall be with child, and shall bring forth a son, and they shall call his name Emmanuel. MATTHEW 1:22–23

And so it was, that, while they were there, the days were accomplished that she should be delivered. And she brought forth her firstborn son, and wrapped him in swaddling clothes, and laid him in a manger; because there was no room for them in the inn. LUKE 2:6–7

75) Shadrach, Meshach, and Abednego

If it be so, our God whom we serve is able to deliver us from the burning fiery furnace, and he will deliver us out of thine hand, O king. But if not, be it known unto thee, O king, that we will not serve thy gods, nor worship the golden image which thou hast set up. DANIEL 3:17–18

And the princes, governors, and captains, and the king's counsellors, being gathered together, saw these men, upon whose bodies the fire had no power, nor was an hair of their head singed, neither were their coats changed, nor the smell of fire had passed on them. DANIEL 3:27

76) Mysterious Creatures

Behold now behemoth, which I made with thee; he eateth grass as an ox. JOB 40:15

In that day the LORD with his sore and great and strong sword shall punish leviathan the piercing serpent, even leviathan that crooked serpent; and he shall slay the dragon that is in the sea. ISAIAH 27:1

77) The Fall of Jericho

And they utterly destroyed all that was in the city, both man and woman, young and old, and ox, and sheep, and ass, with the edge of the sword. JOSHUA 6:21

And it shall come to pass, that when they make a long blast with the ram's horn, and when ye hear the sound of the trumpet, all the people shall shout with a great shout; and the wall of the city shall fall down flat, and the people shall ascend up every man straight before him. JOSHUA 6:5

78) Hosea

Then said the LORD unto me, Go yet, love a woman beloved of her friend, yet an adulteress, according to the love of the LORD toward the children of Israel, who look to other gods, and love flagons of wine. HOSEA 3:1

I will heal their backsliding, I will love them freely: for mine anger is turned away from him. I will be as the dew unto Israel: He shall grow as the lily, and cast forth his roots as Lebanon. HOSEA 14:4–5

79) Money, Money, Money

And Abraham hearkened unto Ephron; and Abraham weighed to Ephron the silver, which he had named in the audience of the sons of Heth, four hundred shekels of silver, current money with the merchant. GENESIS 23:16

And Jesus sat over against the treasury, and beheld how the people cast money into the treasury: and many that were rich cast in much. And there came a certain poor widow, and she threw in two mites, which make a farthing. MARK 12:41–42

80) Get Saved!

For with the heart man believeth unto righteousness; and with the mouth confession is made unto salvation. ROMANS 10:10

Wherefore, my beloved, as ye have always obeyed, not as in my presence only, but now much more in my absence, work out your own salvation with fear and trembling. PHILIPPIANS 2:12

81) Letter to Thessalonica

Now God himself and our Father, and our Lord Jesus Christ, direct our way unto you. And the Lord make you to increase and abound in love one toward another, and toward all men,

even as we do toward you. 1 THESSALONIANS 3:11–12

Now we exhort you, brethren, warn them that are unruly, comfort the feebleminded, support the weak, be patient toward all men. See that none render evil for evil unto any man; but ever follow that which is good, both among yourselves, and to all men. 1 THESSALONIANS 5:14–15

82) Familiar Phrases

Keep me as the apple of the eye, hide me under the shadow of thy wings. PSALM 17:8

Thy watchmen shall lift up the voice; with the voice together shall they sing: for they shall see eye to eye, when the LORD shall bring again Zion. ISAIAH 52:8

83) More Familiar Phrases

Who is he that will plead with me? For now, if I hold my tongue, I shall give up the ghost. JOB 13:19

To the weak became I as weak, that I might gain the weak: I am made all things to all men, that I might by all means save some. 1 CORINTHIANS 9:22

84) You Swine!

And he said unto them, Go. And when they were come out, they went into the herd of swine: and, behold, the whole herd of swine ran violently down a steep place into the sea, and perished in the waters. MATTHEW 8:32

As a jewel of gold in a swine's snout, so is a fair woman which is without discretion. PROVERBS 11:22

85) Mounts and Mountains

And the ark rested in the seventh month, on the seventeenth day of the month, upon the mountains of Ararat. And the waters decreased continually until the tenth month: in the tenth month, on the first day of the month, were the tops of the mountains seen. GENESIS 8:4–5

Gather to me all Israel unto mount Carmel, and the prophets of Baal four hundred and fifty, and the prophets of the groves four hundred, which eat at Jezebel's table. So Ahab sent unto all the children of Israel, and gathered the prophets. 1 KINGS 18:19–20

86) Bible Occupations

Send therefore to Joppa, and call hither Simon, whose surname is Peter; he is lodged in the house of one Simon a tanner by the sea side: who, when he cometh, shall speak unto thee. ACTS 10:32

When Jesus heard it, he saith unto them, They that are whole have no need of the physician, but they that are sick: I came not to call the righteous, but sinners to repentance. MARK 2:17

87) More Bible Occupations

Then answered Amos, and said to Amaziah, I was no prophet, neither was I a prophet's son; but I was an herdman, and a gatherer of sycomore fruit. AMOS 7:14

Demetrius, a silversmith, which made silver shrines for Diana, brought no small gain unto the craftsmen; whom he called together with the workmen of like occupation, and said, Sirs, ye know that by this craft we have our wealth. ACTS 19:24–25

88) Even More Bible Occupations

Be ye ashamed, O ye husbandmen; howl, O ye vinedressers, for the wheat and for the barley; because the harvest of the field is perished. JOEL 1:11

And Jesus said unto the centurion, Go thy way; and as thou hast believed, so be it done unto thee. And his servant was healed in the selfsame hour. MATTHEW 8:13

89) Theological Terms

Therefore as by the offence of one judgment came upon all men to condemnation; even so by the righteousness of one the free gift came upon all men unto justification of life. ROMANS 5:18

Elect according to the foreknowledge of God the Father, through sanctification of the Spirit, unto obedience and sprinkling of the blood of Jesus Christ: Grace unto you, and peace, be multiplied. 1 PETER 1:2

90) Strong Women

Then Jael Heber's wife took a nail of the tent, and took an hammer in her hand, and went softly unto him, and smote the nail into his temples, and fastened it into the ground: for he was fast asleep and weary. So he died. JUDGES 4:21

And Deborah, a prophetess, the wife of Lapidoth, she judged Israel at that time. And she dwelt under the palm tree of Deborah between Ramah and Bethel in mount Ephraim: and the children of Israel came up to her for judgment. JUDGES 4:4–5

91) Nehemiah's Story, Part 1

And I said unto the king, If it please the king, and if thy servant have found favour in thy sight, that thou wouldest send me unto Judah, unto the city of my fathers' sepulchres, that I may build it. NEHEMIAH 2:5

O LORD, I beseech thee, let now thine ear be attentive to the prayer of thy servant, and to the prayer of thy servants, who desire to fear thy name: and prosper, I pray thee, thy servant this day, and grant him mercy in the sight of this man. For I was the king's cupbearer. NEHEMIAH 1:11

92) Nehemiah's Story, Part 2

They which builded on the wall, and they that bare burdens, with those that laded, every one with one of his hands wrought in the work, and with the other hand held a weapon. NEHEMIAH 4:17

So the wall was finished. . . . And it came to pass, that when all our enemies heard thereof, and all the heathen that were about us saw these things, they were much cast down in their own eyes: for they perceived that this work was wrought of our God. NEHEMIAH 6:15–16

93) Repent!

From that time Jesus began to preach, and to say, Repent: for the kingdom of heaven is at hand. MATTHEW 4:17

As I live, saith the Lord GOD, I have no pleasure in the death of the wicked; but that the wicked turn from his way and live. EZEKIEL 33:11

94) Named Angels

And there was war in heaven: Michael and his angels fought against the dragon; and the dragon fought and his angels. REVELATION 12:7

And the angel answering said unto him, I am Gabriel, that stand in the presence of God; and am sent to speak unto thee, and to shew thee these glad tidings. LUKE 1:19

95) Big Cats

And so it was at the beginning of their dwelling there, that they feared not the LORD: therefore the LORD sent lions among them, which slew some of them. 2 KINGS 17:25

And when the prophet that brought him back from the way heard thereof, he said, It is the man of God, who was disobedient unto the word of the LORD: Therefore the LORD hath delivered him unto the lion, which hath torn him, and slain him. 1 KINGS 13:26

96) Scripture on Scripture

For the word of God is quick, and powerful, and sharper than any twoedged sword, piercing even to the dividing asunder of soul and spirit, and of the joints and marrow, and is a discerner of the thoughts and intents of the heart. HEBREWS 4:12

Knowing this first, that no prophecy of the scripture is of any private interpretation. For the prophecy came not in old time by the will of man: But holy men of God spake as they were moved by the Holy Ghost. 2 PETER 1:20–21

97) Off to School

Wherefore the law was our schoolmaster to bring us unto Christ, that we might be justified by faith. But after that faith is come, we are no longer under a schoolmaster. GALATIANS 3:24–25

But when divers were hardened, and believed not, but spake evil of that way before the multitude, he departed from them, and separated the disciples, disputing daily in the school of one Tyrannus. ACTS 19:9

98) Elect Me!

For the children being not yet born, neither having done any good or evil, that the purpose of God according to election might stand, not of works, but of him that calleth. ROMANS 9:11

Wherefore the rather, brethren, give diligence to make your calling and election sure: for if ye do these things, ye shall never fall: For so an entrance shall be ministered unto you abundantly into the everlasting kingdom of our Lord and Saviour Jesus Christ. 2 PETER 1:10–11

99) Tools in the Bible

And on all hills that shall be digged with the mattock, there shall not come thither the fear of briers and thorns: but it shall be for the sending forth of oxen, and for the treading of lesser cattle. ISAIAH 7:25

And the house, when it was in building, was built of stone made ready before it was brought thither: so that there was neither hammer nor axe nor any tool of iron heard in the house, while it was in building. 1 KINGS 6:7

100) The Life of Peter

And when Peter was come down out of the ship, he walked on the water, to go to Jesus. MATTHEW 14:29

Then Peter said, Silver and gold have I none; but such as I have give I thee; In the name of Jesus Christ of Nazareth rise up and walk. ACTS 3:6

101) God's People

If my people, which are called by my name, shall humble themselves, and pray, and seek my face, and turn from their wicked ways; then will I hear from heaven, and will forgive their sin, and will heal their land. 2 CHRONICLES 7:14

But ye are a chosen generation, a royal priesthood, an holy nation, a peculiar people. 1 PETER 2:9

102) Sacrifices

And Abraham took the wood of the burnt offering, and laid it upon Isaac his son; and he took the fire in his hand, and a knife; and they went both of them together. GENESIS 22:6

By the which will we are sanctified through the offering of the body of Jesus Christ once for all. HEBREWS 10:10

103) Not Man's Best Friend

And of Jezebel also spake the LORD, saying, The dogs shall eat Jezebel by the wall of Jezreel. 1 KINGS 21:23

For dogs have compassed me: The assembly of the wicked have inclosed me: They pierced my hands and my feet. PSALM 22:16

104) The Awesomeness of God, Part 1

Who is the blessed and only Potentate, the King of kings, and Lord of lords; who only hath

immortality, dwelling in the light which no man can approach unto; whom no man hath seen, nor can see: to whom be honour and power everlasting. 1 TIMOTHY 6:15–16

For thus saith the high and lofty One that inhabiteth eternity, whose name is Holy; I dwell in the high and holy place, with him also that is of a contrite and humble spirit. ISAIAH 57:15

105) The Awesomeness of God, Part 2

Then said I, Woe is me! For I am undone; because I am a man of unclean lips, and I dwell in the midst of a people of unclean lips: for mine eyes have seen the King, the LORD of hosts. ISAIAH 6:5

I am Alpha and Omega, the beginning and the ending, saith the Lord, which is, and which was, and which is to come, the Almighty. REVELATION 1:8

106) Scenes by the River

If they will not believe also these two signs, neither hearken unto thy voice, that thou shalt take of the water of the river, and pour it upon the dry land: And the water which thou takest out of the river shall become blood upon the dry land. EXODUS 4:9

Rabbi, he that was with thee beyond Jordan, to whom thou barest witness, behold, the same baptizeth, and all men come to him. John answered and said, A man can receive nothing, except it be given him from heaven. JOHN 3:26–27

107) An Even Dozen

All these are the twelve tribes of Israel: and this is it that their father spake unto them, and blessed them; every one. GENESIS 49:28

And it came to pass afterward, that he went throughout every city and village, preaching and shewing the glad tidings of the kingdom of God: and the twelve were with him. LUKE 8:1

108) The Story of Zacchaeus

And he sought to see Jesus who he was; and could not for the press, because he was little of stature. And he ran before, and climbed up into a sycomore tree to see him: for he was to pass that way. LUKE 19:3–4

And Jesus said unto him, This day is salvation come to this house, forsomuch as he also is a son of Abraham. For the Son of man is come to seek and to save that which was lost. LUKE 19:9–10

109) Moses' Sister

And the cloud departed from off the tabernacle; and, behold, Miriam became leprous, white as snow: and Aaron looked upon Miriam, and, behold, she was leprous. NUMBERS 12:10

And Miriam the prophetess, the sister of Aaron, took a timbrel in her hand; and all the women went out after her with timbrels and with dances. And Miriam answered them, Sing ye to the LORD, for he hath triumphed gloriously. EXODUS 15:20–21

110) Cows in the Bible

And God made the beast of the earth after his kind, and cattle after their kind, and every thing that creepeth upon the earth after his kind: and God saw that it was good. GENESIS 1:25

And the LORD shall make thee plenteous in goods, in the fruit of thy body, and in the fruit of thy cattle, and in the fruit of thy ground, in the land which the LORD sware unto thy fathers to give thee. DEUTERONOMY 28:11

111) Holy, Holy, Holy

O God, thou art terrible out of thy holy places: the God of Israel is he that giveth strength and power unto his people. Blessed be God. PSALM 68:35

And when the LORD saw that he turned aside to see, God called unto him out of the midst of the bush, and said, Moses, Moses. And he said, Here am I. And he said, Draw not nigh hither: put off thy shoes from off thy feet, for the place whereon thou standest is holy ground. EXODUS 3:4–5

112) Makin' Music

Speaking to yourselves in psalms and hymns and spiritual songs, singing and making melody in your heart to the Lord; giving thanks always for all things unto God. EPHESIANS 5:19–20

As the trumpeters and singers were as one, to make one sound to be heard in praising and thanking the LORD; and when they lifted up their voice with the trumpets and cymbals and instruments of musick, and praised the LORD, saying, For he is good; for his mercy endureth for ever: that then the house was filled with a cloud. 2 CHRONICLES 5:13

113) Bones

And Moses took the bones of Joseph with him: for he had straitly sworn the children of Israel, saying, God will surely visit you; and ye shall carry up my bones away hence with you. EXODUS 13:19

They arose, all the valiant men, and took away the body of Saul, and the bodies of his sons, and brought them to Jabesh, and buried their bones under the oak in Jabesh, and fasted seven days. 1 CHRONICLES 10:12

114) From Psalm 119

With my lips have I declared all the judgments of thy mouth. I have rejoiced in the way of thy testimonies, as much as in all riches. I will meditate in thy precepts, and have respect unto thy ways. PSALM 119:13–15

Give me understanding, and I shall keep thy law; yea, I shall observe it with my whole heart. Make me to go in the path of thy commandments; for therein do I delight. PSALM 119:34–35

115) More from Psalm 119

The earth, O LORD, is full of thy mercy: teach me thy statutes. Thou hast dealt well with thy servant, O LORD, according unto thy word. Teach me good judgment and knowledge: for I have believed thy commandments. PSALM 119:64–66

The wicked have laid a snare for me: yet I erred not from thy precepts. Thy testimonies have I taken as an heritage for ever: for they are the rejoicing of my heart. I have inclined mine heart to perform thy statutes alway, even unto the end. PSALM 119:110–112

116) Giant Trouble

And there went out a champion out of the camp of the Philistines, named Goliath, of Gath, whose height was six cubits and a span. 1 SAMUEL 17:4

And yet again there was war at Gath, where was a man of great stature, whose fingers and toes were four and twenty, six on each hand, and six on each foot and he also was the son of the giant. 1 CHRONICLES 20:6

117) New Testament Rulers

Now when Jesus was born in Bethlehem of Judaea in the days of Herod the king, behold, there came wise men from the east to Jerusalem. MATTHEW 2:1

And Jesus answering said unto them, Render to Caesar the things that are Caesar's, and to God the things that are God's. MARK 12:17

118) A Babylonian King

Then Nebuchadnezzar the king sent to gather together the princes, the governors, and the captains, the judges, the treasurers, the counsellors, the sheriffs, and all the rulers of the provinces, to come to the dedication of the image which Nebuchadnezzar the king had set up. DANIEL 3:2

Then Nebuchadnezzar spake, and said, Blessed be the God of Shadrach, Meshach, and Abednego, who hath sent his angel, and delivered his servants that trusted in him, and have changed the king's word. DANIEL 3:28

119) Rules for Church Leaders

A bishop then must be blameless, the husband of one wife, vigilant, sober, of good behaviour, given to hospitality, apt to teach; not given to wine, no striker, not greedy of filthy lucre; but patient, not a brawler, not covetous. 1 TIMOTHY 3:2–3

Then the twelve called the multitude of the disciples unto them, and said, It is not reason that we should leave the word of God, and serve tables. Wherefore, brethren, look ye out among you seven men of honest report, full of the Holy Ghost and wisdom. ACTS 6:2–3

120) Spiritual U-Turns

Say unto them, As I live, saith the Lord GOD, I have no pleasure in the death of the wicked; but that the wicked turn from his way and live: turn ye, turn ye from your evil ways; for why will ye die, O house of Israel? EZEKIEL 33:11

Turn, O backsliding children, saith the LORD; for I am married unto you: and I will take you one of a city, and two of a family, and I will bring you to Zion. JEREMIAH 3:14

121) Hellish Stuff

And if thy hand offend thee, cut it off: it is better for thee to enter into life maimed, than having two hands to go into hell, into the fire that never shall be quenched: where their worm dieth not, and the fire is not quenched. MARK 9:43–44

And the beast was taken, and with him the false prophet that wrought miracles before him, with which he deceived them that had received the mark of the beast, and them that worshipped his image. These both were cast alive into a lake of fire burning with brimstone. REVELATION 19:20

122) More Hellish Stuff

But the fearful, and unbelieving, and the abominable, and murderers, and whoremongers, and sorcerers, and idolaters, and all liars, shall have their part in the lake which burneth with fire and brimstone: which is the second death. REVELATION 21:8

Send Lazarus, that he may dip the tip of his finger in water, and cool my tongue; for I am tormented in this flame. But Abraham said, Son, remember that thou in thy lifetime receivedst thy good things, and likewise Lazarus evil things: but now he is comforted, and thou art tormented. LUKE 16:24–25

123) Heavenly Stuff

And he said unto Jesus, Lord, remember me when thou comest into thy kingdom. And Jesus said unto him, Verily I say unto thee, Today shalt thou be with me in paradise. LUKE 23:42–43

And I knew such a man, (whether in the body, or out of the body, I cannot tell: God knoweth;) how that he was caught up into paradise, and heard unspeakable words, which it is not lawful for a man to utter. 2 CORINTHIANS 12:3–4

124) More Heavenly Stuff

Him that overcometh will I make a pillar in the temple of my God, and he shall go no more out: and I will write upon him the name of my God, and the name of the city of my God, which is new Jerusalem, which cometh down out of heaven from my God: and I will write upon him my new name. REVELATION 3:12

Now when all the people were baptized, it came to pass, that Jesus also being baptized, and

praying, the heaven was opened, and the Holy Ghost descended in a bodily shape like a dove upon him, and a voice came from heaven, which said, Thou art my beloved Son. LUKE 3:21–22

125) Lesser-Known Disciples

Judas saith unto him, not Iscariot, Lord, how is it that thou wilt manifest thyself unto us, and not unto the world? JOHN 14:22

We have found him, of whom Moses in the law, and the prophets, did write, Jesus of Nazareth, the son of Joseph. And Nathanael said unto him, Can there any good thing come out of Nazareth? Philip saith unto him, Come and see. JOHN 1:45–46

126) Biblical Horses

For the horse of Pharaoh went in with his chariots and with his horsemen into the sea, and the LORD brought again the waters of the sea upon them; but the children of Israel went on dry land in the midst of the sea. EXODUS 15:19

And number thee an army, like the army that thou hast lost, horse for horse, and chariot for chariot: and we will fight against them in the plain, and surely we shall be stronger than they. And he hearkened unto their voice, and did so. 1 KINGS 20:25

127) Villains

Alexander the coppersmith did me much evil: the Lord reward him according to his works: of whom be thou ware also; for he hath greatly withstood our words. 2 TIMOTHY 4:14–15

And he thought scorn to lay hands on Mordecai alone; for they had shewed him the people of Mordecai: wherefore Haman sought to destroy all the Jews that were throughout the whole kingdom of Ahasuerus, even the people of Mordecai. ESTHER 3:6

128) Noah's Ark

And this is the fashion which thou shalt make it of: The length of the ark shall be three hundred cubits, the breadth of it fifty cubits, and the height of it thirty cubits. GENESIS 6:15

There went in two and two unto Noah into the ark, the male and the female, as God had commanded Noah. GENESIS 7:9

129) Executions

And she, being before instructed of her mother, said, Give me here John Baptist's head in a charger. MATTHEW 14:8

So they hanged Haman on the gallows that he had prepared for Mordecai. Then was the king's wrath pacified. ESTHER 7:10

130) Fish Fry

These ye shall eat of all that are in the waters: all that have fins and scales shall ye eat. DEUTERONOMY 14:9

As soon then as they were come to land, they saw a fire of coals there, and fish laid thereon, and bread. JOHN 21:9

131) Planting and Harvesting

They have sown wheat, but shall reap thorns: they have put themselves to pain, but shall not profit: and they shall be ashamed of your revenues because of the fierce anger of the LORD. JEREMIAH 12:13

Be not deceived; God is not mocked: for whatsoever a man soweth, that shall he also reap. For he that soweth to his flesh shall of the flesh reap corruption; but he that soweth to the Spirit shall of the Spirit reap life everlasting. GALATIANS 6:7–8

132) Other Farm Analogies

Whose fan is in his hand, and he will throughly purge his floor, and gather his wheat into the garner; but he will burn up the

chaff with unquenchable fire.
MATTHEW 3:12

Put ye in the sickle, for the harvest
is ripe: come, get you down; for
the press is full, the fats overflow;
for their wickedness is great.
JOEL 3:13

133) Athletics in the Bible
I therefore so run, not as
uncertainly; so fight I, not as one
that beateth the air: But I keep
under my body, and bring it into
subjection: lest that by any means,
when I have preached to others, I
myself should be a castaway.
1 CORINTHIANS 9:26–27

Wherefore seeing we also are
compassed about with so great a
cloud of witnesses, let us lay aside
every weight, and the sin which
doth so easily beset us, and let us
run with patience the race that is
set before us. HEBREWS 12:1

134) Weaponry
And the LORD said unto Joshua,
Stretch out the spear that is in thy
hand toward Ai; for I will give
it into thine hand. And Joshua
stretched out the spear that he
had in his hand toward the city.
JOSHUA 8:18

Whose arrows are sharp, and all
their bows bent, their horses'
hoofs shall be counted like flint,
and their wheels like a whirlwind.
ISAIAH 5:28

135) How Big Is God?
Am I a God at hand, saith the
LORD, and not a God afar off?
Can any hide himself in secret
places that I shall not see him?
saith the LORD. Do not I fill
heaven and earth? saith the LORD.
JEREMIAH 23:23–24

Whither shall I go from thy
spirit? or whither shall I flee from
thy presence? If I ascend up into
heaven, thou art there: if I make
my bed in hell, behold, thou art
there. PSALM 139:7–8

136) Biblical Kisses
Mercy and truth are met together;
righteousness and peace have
kissed each other. PSALM 85:10

When Jacob saw Rachel the
daughter of Laban his mother's
brother, and the sheep of Laban his
mother's brother, that Jacob went
near, and rolled the stone from
the well's mouth, and watered the
flock of Laban his mother's brother.
And Jacob kissed Rachel. GENESIS
29:10–11

137) Honesty Is the Best Policy
A false balance is abomination to
the LORD: But a just weight is his
delight. PROVERBS 11:1

And that ye put on the new man,
which after God is created in
righteousness and true holiness.
Wherefore putting away lying,
speak every man truth with his
neighbour: for we are members
one of another. EPHESIANS 4:24–25

138) Battle Scenes
And the LORD delivered it also,
and the king thereof, into the
hand of Israel; and he smote it
with the edge of the sword, and
all the souls that were therein; he
let none remain in it; but did unto
the king thereof as he did unto the
king of Jericho. JOSHUA 10:30

The kings came and fought,
then fought the kings of Canaan
in Taanach by the waters of
Megiddo; they took no gain of
money. They fought from heaven;
the stars in their courses fought
against Sisera. Judges 5:19–20

139) Ancient Places
And he said unto him, I am the
LORD that brought thee out of Ur
of the Chaldees, to give thee this
land to inherit it. GENESIS 15:7

There was a man in the land of
Uz, whose name was Job; and
that man was perfect and upright,
and one that feared God, and
eschewed evil. JOB 1:1

140) Crazy, Man
And David laid up these words
in his heart, and was sore afraid
of Achish the king of Gath. And
he changed his behaviour before
them, and feigned himself mad
in their hands, and scrabbled on
the doors of the gate, and let his
spittle fall down upon his beard.
1 SAMUEL 21:12–13

Festus said with a loud voice, Paul,
thou art beside thyself; much
learning doth make thee mad. But
he said, I am not mad, most noble
Festus; but speak forth the words of
truth and soberness. ACTS 26:24–25

141) Children of the Bible
And now, little children, abide in
him; that, when he shall appear,
we may have confidence, and
not be ashamed before him at his
coming. 1 JOHN 2:28

Then were there brought unto him
little children, that he should put
his hands on them, and pray: and
the disciples rebuked them. But
Jesus said, Suffer little children,
and forbid them not, to come unto
me: for of such is the kingdom of
heaven. MATTHEW 19:13–14

142) It's Magic
There shall not be found among
you any one that maketh his
son or his daughter to pass
through the fire, or that useth
divination, or an observer of
times, or an enchanter, or a witch.
DEUTERONOMY 18:10

A man also or woman that hath a
familiar spirit, or that is a wizard,
shall surely be put to death: they
shall stone them with stones:
their blood shall be upon them.
LEVITICUS 20:27

143) Craftsmanship
Cursed be the man that maketh
any graven or molten image, an
abomination unto the LORD,
the work of the hands of the
craftsman, and putteth it in a
secret place. And all the people

shall answer and say, Amen.
DEUTERONOMY 27:15

And the voice of harpers, and musicians, and of pipers, and trumpeters, shall be heard no more at all in thee; and no craftsman, of whatsoever craft he be, shall be found any more in thee; and the sound of a millstone shall be heard no more at all in thee. REVELATION 18:22

144) God's Love

For when we were yet without strength, in due time Christ died for the ungodly. ROMANS 5:6

For I am persuaded, that neither death, nor life, nor angels, nor principalities, nor powers, nor things present, nor things to come, nor height, nor depth, nor any other creature, shall be able to separate us from the love of God, which is in Christ Jesus our Lord. ROMANS 8:38–39

145) On the Vine

Abide in me, and I in you. As the branch cannot bear fruit of itself, except it abide in the vine; no more can ye, except ye abide in me. JOHN 15:4

(For the fruit of the Spirit is in all goodness and righteousness and truth;) proving what is acceptable unto the Lord. EPHESIANS 5:9–10

146) Jesus Describes Himself

Then spake Jesus again unto them, saying, I am the light of the world: he that followeth me shall not walk in darkness, but shall have the light of life. JOHN 8:12

I am the door: by me if any man enter in, he shall be saved, and shall go in and out, and find pasture. The thief cometh not, but for to steal, and to kill, and to destroy: I am come that they might have life, and that they might have it more abundantly. JOHN 10:9–10

147) Paul Describes Himself

He cried out in the council, Men and brethren, I am a Pharisee, the son of a Pharisee: of the hope and resurrection of the dead I am called in question. ACTS 23:6

Circumcised the eighth day, of the stock of Israel, of the tribe of Benjamin, an Hebrew of the Hebrews; as touching the law, a Pharisee; concerning zeal, persecuting the church; touching the righteousness which is in the law, blameless. PHILIPPIANS 3:5–6

148) I'm Depressed

And it came to pass, when the sun did arise, that God prepared a vehement east wind; and the sun beat upon the head of Jonah, that he fainted, and wished in himself to die, and said, It is better for me to die than to live. JONAH 4:8

But he himself went a day's journey into the wilderness, and came and sat down under a juniper tree: and he requested for himself that he might die; and said, It is enough; now, O LORD, take away my life; for I am not better than my fathers. 1 KINGS 19:4

149) I'm Full of Joy

I will bless the LORD at all times: his praise shall continually be in my mouth. My soul shall make her boast in the LORD: the humble shall hear thereof, and be glad. PSALM 34:1–2

And Mary said, My soul doth magnify the Lord, and my spirit hath rejoiced in God my Saviour. For he hath regarded the low estate of his handmaiden: For, behold, from henceforth all generations shall call me blessed. LUKE 1:46–48

150) Solar Occurrences

And the sun stood still, and the moon stayed, until the people had avenged themselves upon their enemies. Is not this written in the book of Jasher? So the sun stood still in the midst of heaven. JOSHUA 10:13

And it was about the sixth hour, and there was a darkness over all the earth until the ninth hour. And the sun was darkened, and the veil of the temple was rent in the midst. And when Jesus had cried with a loud voice, he said, Father, into thy hands I commend my spirit. LUKE 23:44–46

151) Let's Party

And when these days were expired, the king made a feast unto all the people that were present in Shushan the palace, both unto great and small, seven days, in the court of the garden of the king's palace. ESTHER 1:5

When thou makest a dinner or a supper, call not thy friends, nor thy brethren, neither thy kinsmen, nor thy rich neighbours; lest they also bid thee again, and a recompence be made thee. But when thou makest a feast, call the poor, the maimed, the lame, the blind: And thou shalt be blessed. LUKE 14:12–14

152) Protected

The night is far spent, the day is at hand: let us therefore cast off the works of darkness, and let us put on the armour of light. ROMANS 13:12

Put on the whole armour of God, that ye may be able to stand against the wiles of the devil. For we wrestle not against flesh and blood, but against principalities, against powers, against the rulers of the darkness of this world, against spiritual wickedness in high places. EPHESIANS 6:11–12

153) Famous Names

By faith Abraham, when he was called to go out into a place which he should after receive for an inheritance, obeyed; and he went out, not knowing whither he went. HEBREWS 11:8

Then went king David in, and sat before the LORD, and he said, Who am I, O Lord GOD? and what is my house, that thou hast brought me hitherto? 2 SAMUEL 7:18

154) More Famous Names

And king Solomon shall be blessed, and the throne of David shall be established before the LORD for ever. 1 KINGS 2:45

Then Jonathan and David made a covenant, because he loved him as his own soul. 1 SAMUEL 18:3

155) The Temptation of Christ

And Jesus being full of the Holy Ghost returned from Jordan, and was led by the Spirit into the wilderness, being forty days tempted of the devil. And in those days he did eat nothing. LUKE 4:1–2

All this power will I give thee, and the glory of them: for that is delivered unto me; and to whomsoever I will I give it. If thou therefore wilt worship me, all shall be thine. And Jesus answered and said unto him, Get thee behind me, Satan: for it is written, Thou shalt worship the Lord thy God. LUKE 4:6–8

156) The Avenger

To me belongeth vengeance and recompence; their foot shall slide in due time: for the day of their calamity is at hand, and the things that shall come upon them make haste. DEUTERONOMY 32:35

Say to them that are of a fearful heart, Be strong, fear not: behold, your God will come with vengeance, even God with a recompence; he will come and save you. ISAIAH 35:4

157) Valuables

But lay up for yourselves treasures in heaven, where neither moth nor rust doth corrupt, and where thieves do not break through nor steal: For where your treasure is, there will your heart be also. MATTHEW 6:20–21

But God said unto him, Thou fool, this night thy soul shall be required of thee: Then whose shall those things be, which thou hast provided? So is he that layeth up treasure for himself, and is not rich toward God. LUKE 12:20–21

158) Dazed and Confused

And they were all amazed, insomuch that they questioned among themselves, saying, What thing is this? what new doctrine is this? for with authority commandeth he even the unclean spirits, and they do obey him. MARK 1:27

The multitude came together, and were confounded, because that every man heard them speak in his own language. And they were all amazed and marvelled, saying one to another, Behold, are not all these which speak Galilaeans? And how hear we every man in our own tongue? ACTS 2:6–8

159) The Shepherd

But when he saw the multitudes, he was moved with compassion on them, because they fainted, and were scattered abroad, as sheep having no shepherd. MATTHEW 9:36

I am the good shepherd, and know my sheep, and am known of mine. As the Father knoweth me, even so know I the Father: and I lay down my life for the sheep. JOHN 10:14–15

160) Fruit of the Vine

Do not drink wine nor strong drink, thou, nor thy sons with thee, when ye go into the tabernacle of the congregation, lest ye die: it shall be a statute for ever throughout your generations. LEVITICUS 10:9

Restore, I pray you, to them, even this day, their lands, their vineyards, their oliveyards, and their houses, also the hundredth part of the money, and of the corn, the wine, and the oil, that ye exact of them. NEHEMIAH 5:11

161) Love Songs

As the apple tree among the trees of the wood, so is my beloved among the sons. I sat down under his shadow with great delight, and his fruit was sweet to my taste. SONG OF SOLOMON 2:3

How fair is thy love, my sister, my spouse! how much better is thy love than wine! and the smell of thine ointments than all spices! SONG OF SOLOMON 4:10

162) Introducing Peter's Brother

And Jesus, walking by the sea of Galilee, saw two brethren, Simon called Peter, and Andrew his brother, casting a net into the sea: for they were fishers.MATTHEW 4:18

One of his disciples, Andrew, Simon Peter's brother, saith unto him, There is a lad here, which hath five barley loaves, and two small fishes: but what are they among so many? JOHN 6:8–9

163) Mysteries

There be three things which are too wonderful for me, yea, four which I know not: the way of an eagle in the air; the way of a serpent upon a rock; the way of a ship in the midst of the sea; and the way of a man with a maid. PROVERBS 30:18–19

Behold, I shew you a mystery; we shall not all sleep, but we shall all be changed, in a moment, in the twinkling of an eye, at the last trump: for the trumpet shall sound, and the dead shall be raised incorruptible, and we shall be changed. 1 CORINTHIANS 15:51–52

164) Victory!

These shall make war with the Lamb, and the Lamb shall overcome them: for he is Lord of lords, and King of kings: And they that are with him are called, and chosen, and faithful. REVELATION 17:14

These things I have spoken unto you, that in me ye might have peace. In the world ye shall have tribulation: but be of good cheer; I have overcome the world. JOHN 16:33

165) The Patriarchs, Part 1

Neither shall thy name any more be called Abram, but thy name shall be Abraham; for a father of many nations have I made thee. GENESIS 17:5

I am the God of Abraham thy father: fear not, for I am with thee, and will bless thee, and multiply thy seed for my servant Abraham's sake. And he builded an altar there, and called upon the name of the LORD, and pitched his tent there. GENESIS 26:24–25

166) The Patriarchs, Part 2

Behold, I have set the land before you: go in and possess the land which the LORD sware unto your fathers, Abraham, Isaac, and Jacob, to give unto them and to their seed after them. DEUTERONOMY 1:8

And Jacob vowed a vow, saying, If God will be with me, and will keep me in this way that I go, and will give me bread to eat, and raiment to put on, so that I come again to my father's house in peace; then shall the LORD be my God. GENESIS 28:20–21

167) Stormy Weather

And, behold, there came a great wind from the wilderness, and smote the four corners of the house, and it fell upon the young men, and they are dead; and I only am escaped alone to tell thee. JOB 1:19

Behold, the LORD passed by, and a great strong wind rent the mountains, and brake in pieces the rocks before the LORD; but the LORD was not in the wind: and after the wind an earthquake; but the LORD was not in the earthquake. 1 KINGS 19:11

168) Raised from the Dead

But Peter put them all forth, and kneeled down, and prayed; and turning him to the body said, Tabitha, arise. And she opened her eyes: and when she saw Peter, she sat up. And he gave her his hand, and lifted her up, and when he had called the saints and widows, presented her alive. ACTS 9:40–41

And as Paul was long preaching, he sunk down with sleep, and fell down from the third loft, and was taken up dead. And Paul went down, and fell on him, and embracing him said, Trouble not yourselves; for his life is in him. ACTS 20:9–10

169) Taking an Offering

Every man according as he purposeth in his heart, so let him give; not grudgingly, or of necessity: for God loveth a cheerful giver. 2 CORINTHIANS 9:7

Bring ye all the tithes into the storehouse, that there may be meat in mine house, and prove me now herewith, saith the LORD of hosts, if I will not open you the windows of heaven, and pour you out a blessing, that there shall not be room enough to receive it. MALACHI 3:10

170) Quotable Ezra

All such as had separated themselves unto them from the filthiness of the heathen of the land, to seek the LORD God of Israel, did eat, and kept the feast of unleavened bread seven days with joy. EZRA 6:21–22

But many of the priests and Levites and chief of the fathers, who were ancient men, that had seen the first house, when the foundation of this house was laid before their eyes, wept with a loud voice; and many shouted aloud for joy: So that the people could not discern the noise of the shout of joy from the noise of the weeping of the people. EZRA 3:12–13

171) Troublemakers

And there was no water for the congregation: and they gathered themselves together against Moses and against Aaron. And the people chode with Moses, and spake, saying, Would God that we had died when our brethren died before the LORD! NUMBERS 20:2–3

And the earth opened her mouth, and swallowed them up together with Korah, when that company died, what time the fire devoured two hundred and fifty men: and they became a sign. NUMBERS 26:10

172) The Second Coming

And then shall appear the sign of the Son of man in heaven: and then shall all the tribes of the earth mourn, and they shall see the Son of man coming in the clouds of heaven with power and great glory. MATTHEW 24:30

But of that day and that hour knoweth no man, no, not the angels which are in heaven, neither the Son, but the Father. Take ye heed, watch and pray: for ye know not when the time is. MARK 13:32–33

173) A Common Woman's Name

Is not this the carpenter's son? is not his mother called Mary? and his brethren, James, and Joses, and Simon, and Judas? MATTHEW 13:55

And when the sabbath was past, Mary Magdalene, and Mary the mother of James, and Salome, had bought sweet spices, that they might come and anoint him. MARK 16:1

174) God Provides

Consider the lilies how they grow: they toil not, they spin not; and yet I say unto you, that Solomon in all his glory was not arrayed like one of these. LUKE 12:27

I have been young, and now am old; yet have I not seen the righteous forsaken, nor his seed begging bread. PSALM 37:25

175) Important Questions

Fear ye not, neither be afraid: have not I told thee from that time, and have declared it? Ye are even my witnesses. Is there a God beside me? yea, there is no God; I know not any. ISAIAH 44:8

But when the Pharisees had heard that he had put the Sadducees to silence, they were gathered together. Then one of them, which was a lawyer, asked him a question, tempting him, and saying, Master, which is the great commandment in the law? MATTHEW 22:34–36

176) Martyrs

And they stoned Stephen, calling upon God, and saying, Lord Jesus, receive my spirit. And he kneeled down, and cried with a loud voice, Lord, lay not this sin to their charge. And when he had said this, he fell asleep. ACTS 7:59–60

They were stoned, they were sawn asunder, were tempted, were slain with the sword: they wandered about in sheepskins and goatskins; being destitute, afflicted, tormented; (of whom the world was not worthy). HEBREWS 11:37–38

177) Dreamers

And Pharaoh said unto Joseph, I have dreamed a dream, and there is none that can interpret it: and I have heard say of thee, that thou canst understand a dream to interpret it. GENESIS 41:15

And he told it to his father, and to his brethren: and his father rebuked him, and said unto him, What is this dream that thou hast dreamed? Shall I and thy mother and thy brethren indeed come to bow down ourselves to thee to the earth? GENESIS 37:10

178) A Word from Amos

For, lo, he that formeth the mountains, and createth the wind, and declareth unto man what is his thought, that maketh the morning darkness, and treadeth upon the high places of the earth, The LORD, The God of hosts, is his name. AMOS 4:13

Therefore the flight shall perish from the swift, and the strong shall not strengthen his force, neither shall the mighty deliver himself: neither shall he stand that handleth the bow; and he that is swift of foot shall not deliver himself: neither shall he that rideth the horse deliver himself. AMOS 2:14–15

179) The Opposite of Proud

Notwithstanding Hezekiah humbled himself for the pride of his heart, both he and the inhabitants of Jerusalem, so that the wrath of the LORD came not upon them in the days of Hezekiah. 2 CHRONICLES 32:26

Thou art snared with the words of thy mouth, thou art taken with the words of thy mouth. Do this now, my son, and deliver thyself, when thou art come into the hand of thy friend; go, humble thyself, and make sure thy friend. PROVERBS 6:2–3

180) Guilty!

Now we know that what things soever the law saith, it saith to them who are under the law: that every mouth may be stopped, and all the world may become guilty before God. ROMANS 3:19

But if ye have respect to persons, ye commit sin, and are convinced of the law as transgressors. For whosoever shall keep the whole law, and yet offend in one point, he is guilty of all. JAMES 2:9–10

181) Forgiven!

For as the heaven is high above the earth, so great is his mercy toward them that fear him. As far as the east is from the west, so far hath he removed our transgressions from us. PSALM 103:11–12

If we say that we have fellowship with him, and walk in darkness, we lie, and do not the truth: But if we walk in the light, as he is in the light, we have fellowship one with another, and the blood of Jesus Christ his Son cleanseth us from all sin. 1 JOHN 1:6–7

182) Gossip and Slander

For I fear, lest, when I come, I shall not find you such as I would, and that I shall be found unto you such as ye would not: lest there be debates, envyings, wraths, strifes, backbitings, whisperings, swellings, tumults. 2 CORINTHIANS 12:20

Lord, who shall abide in thy tabernacle? who shall dwell in thy holy hill? He that walketh uprightly, and worketh righteousness, and speaketh the truth in his heart. He that backbiteth not with his tongue, nor doeth evil to his neighbour. PSALM 15:1–3

183) What the World Needs Most

Owe no man any thing, but to love one another: for he that loveth another hath fulfilled the law. ROMANS 13:8

Seeing ye have purified your souls in obeying the truth through the Spirit unto unfeigned love of the brethren, see that ye love one another with a pure heart fervently: being born again, not of corruptible seed, but of incorruptible, by the word of God. 1 PETER 1:22–23

184) Biblical Skyscrapers

Or those eighteen, upon whom the tower in Siloam fell, and slew them, think ye that they were sinners above all men that dwelt in Jerusalem? I tell you, Nay: but, except ye repent, ye shall all likewise perish. LUKE 13:4–5

Go to, let us make brick, and burn them thoroughly. And they had brick for stone, and slime had they for morter. And they said, Go to, let us build us a city and a tower, whose top may reach unto heaven; and let us make us a name, lest we be scattered abroad. GENESIS 11:3–4

185) Advice from James

Even so faith, if it hath not works, is dead, being alone. Yea, a man may say, Thou hast faith, and I have works: shew me thy faith without thy works, and I will shew thee my faith by my works. JAMES 2:17–18

From whence come wars and fightings among you? come they not hence, even of your lusts that war in your members? Ye lust, and have not: ye kill, and desire to have, and cannot obtain: ye fight and war, yet ye have not, because ye ask not. JAMES 4:1–2

186) More Advice from James

Whereas ye know not what shall be on the morrow. For what is your life? It is even a vapour, that appeareth for a little time, and then vanisheth away. For that ye ought to say, If the Lord will, we shall live, and do this, or that. JAMES 4:14–15

Be patient therefore, brethren, unto the coming of the Lord. Behold, the husbandman waiteth for the precious fruit of the earth, and hath long patience for it, until he receive the early and latter rain. Be ye also patient; stablish your hearts: for the coming of the Lord draweth nigh. JAMES 5:7–8

187) Doubting Thomas

Then saith he to Thomas, Reach hither thy finger, and behold my hands; and reach hither thy hand, and thrust it into my side: and be not faithless, but believing. JOHN 20:27

Jesus saith unto him, Thomas, because thou hast seen me, thou hast believed: Blessed are they that have not seen, and yet have believed. JOHN 20:29

188) True Motivation

And whatsoever ye do in word or deed, do all in the name of the Lord Jesus, giving thanks to God and the Father by him. COLOSSIANS 3:17

But thou, O man of God, flee these things; and follow after

righteousness, godliness, faith, love, patience, meekness. 1 TIMOTHY 6:11

189) A Biblical Queen

And when the queen of Sheba heard of the fame of Solomon concerning the name of the LORD, she came to prove him with hard questions. 1 KINGS 10:1

The queen of the south shall rise up in the judgment with the men of this generation, and condemn them: for she came from the utmost parts of the earth to hear the wisdom of Solomon; and, behold, a greater than Solomon is here. LUKE 11:31

190) Trees

And they heard the voice of the LORD God walking in the garden in the cool of the day: and Adam and his wife hid themselves from the presence of the LORD God amongst the trees of the garden. GENESIS 3:8

Thou shalt not plant thee a grove of any trees near unto the altar of the LORD thy God, which thou shalt make thee. DEUTERONOMY 16:21

191) When Life Doesn't Make Sense

For my thoughts are not your thoughts, neither are your ways my ways, saith the LORD. For as the heavens are higher than the earth, so are my ways higher than your ways, and my thoughts than your thoughts. ISAIAH 55:8–9

Then Job answered the LORD, and said, I know that thou canst do every thing, and that no thought can be withholden from thee. Who is he that hideth counsel without knowledge? therefore have I uttered that I understood not; things too wonderful for me, which I knew not. JOB 42:1–3

192) Rock and Roll

Whoso diggeth a pit shall fall therein: and he that rolleth a stone, it will return upon him. PROVERBS 26:27

And, behold, there was a great earthquake: for the angel of the Lord descended from heaven, and came and rolled back the stone from the door, and sat upon it. MATTHEW 28:2

193) What a Waste. . .

Vanity of vanities, saith the Preacher, vanity of vanities; all is vanity. What profit hath a man of all his labour which he taketh under the sun? ECCLESIASTES 1:2–3

For what is a man profited, if he shall gain the whole world, and lose his own soul? or what shall a man give in exchange for his soul? MATTHEW 16:26

194) Gimme a Sign

And Simeon blessed them, and said unto Mary his mother, Behold, this child is set for the fall and rising again of many in Israel; and for a sign which shall be spoken against. LUKE 2:34

But he answered and said unto them, An evil and adulterous generation seeketh after a sign; and there shall no sign be given to it, but the sign of the prophet Jonas. MATTHEW 12:39

195) Bible Study

Search the scriptures; for in them ye think ye have eternal life: and they are they which testify of me. JOHN 5:39

And the brethren immediately sent away Paul and Silas by night unto Berea: who coming thither went into the synagogue of the Jews. These were more noble than those in Thessalonica, in that they received the word with all readiness of mind, and searched the scriptures daily. ACTS 17:10–11

196) God's Wealth

The silver is mine, and the gold is mine, saith the LORD of hosts. HAGGAI 2:8

For every beast of the forest is mine, and the cattle upon a thousand hills. I know all the fowls of the mountains: and the wild beasts of the field are mine. If I were hungry, I would not tell thee: for the world is mine, and the fulness thereof. PSALM 50:10–12

197) Dirty Birds

And these are they which ye shall have in abomination among the fowls; they shall not be eaten, they are an abomination: the eagle, and the ossifrage, and the ospray. LEVITICUS 11:13

I will give thee unto the ravenous birds of every sort, and to the beasts of the field to be devoured. EZEKIEL 39:4

198) Nice Birds

Are not two sparrows sold for a farthing? and one of them shall not fall on the ground without your Father. MATTHEW 10:29

The flowers appear on the earth; the time of the singing of birds is come, and the voice of the turtle is heard in our land. SONG OF SOLOMON 2:12

199) Important Terms

And he is the propitiation for our sins: and not for ours only, but also for the sins of the whole world. 1 JOHN 2:2

Who was delivered for our offences, and was raised again for our justification. ROMANS 4:25

200) Thoughts on Prayer

My voice shalt thou hear in the morning, O LORD; in the morning will I direct my prayer unto thee, and will look up. PSALM 5:3

The sacrifice of the wicked is an abomination to the LORD: but the prayer of the upright is his delight. PROVERBS 15:8

201) Jesus' Power

All things were created by him, and for him: And he is before all things, and by him all things consist. COLOSSIANS 1:16–17

That at the name of Jesus every knee should bow, of things in heaven, and things in earth, and things under the earth. PHILIPPIANS 2:10

202) Saving the Best for Last

Then Simon Peter answered him, Lord, to whom shall we go? thou hast the words of eternal life. JOHN 6:68

Thou wilt shew me the path of life: in thy presence is fulness of joy; at thy right hand there are pleasures for evermore. PSALM 16:11